Coaching the Sale

Coaching the Sale

Discover the Issues, Discuss Solutions and Decide an Outcome!

Tim Ursiny, Ph.D., RCC and Gary DeMoss
with James A. Morel

SOURCEBOOKS, INC.
NAPERVILLE, ILLINOIS

Published by Sourcebooks, Inc.
P.O. Box 4410, Naperville, Illinois 60567-4410
(630) 961-3900
Fax: (630) 961-2168
www.sourcebooks.com

Library of Congress Cataloging-in-Publication Data

Ursiny, Timothy E.
  Coaching the sale : discovering the issues, discussing solutions and
deciding an outcome! / Tim Ursiny, Gary DeMoss, with James Morel.
      p. cm.
  Includes bibliographical references and index.
  ISBN-13: 978-1-4022-0635-1 (alk. paper)
  ISBN-10: 1-4022-0635-6 (alk. paper)
  1. Selling. I. DeMoss, Gary. II. Morel, James. III. Title.

HF5438.25.U77 2006
658.85--dc22

2006014448

Printed and bound in the United States of America.
CH 10 9 8 7 6 5 4 3 2 1

Dedication

From Tim

To a talented leader, a gifted mentor, and a good friend, Keith VanderVeen. I will always be grateful that you inspired me to build a business. To Marla, Zach, Colton, and Vance for their support and love.

From Gary

To my wonderful wife, Laurelyn, who has been most supportive and understanding throughout my travels, and to my children, Brandon, Matt, Jonathan, Leah, Lauren, and Tyler, who bring me my daily doses of joy and challenges.

From Jim

To Sherry for support and love. And to all of the clients who have touched my business life and influenced my thoughts throughout this book.

Acknowledgments

Authors are often only as good as their publisher and we are no exception. Our heartfelt thanks to the entire team at Sourcebooks, including, but not limited to, Peter Lynch, Heather Moore, Sean Murray, Rodney Wachowiak, Anne Landa, Tara VanTimmeren, and the visionary and creative person who brings it all together, Dominique Raccah. You do so much for your authors and we appreciate it greatly.

A special thanks to Mitch Anthony who came up with our subtitle. Mitch, you do magic with words.

Another special thank you to the team at Van Kampen. You have been wonderful business partners and friends and we have learned so much from our relationship with you.

To our clients we can only say thank you for including us in your lives. Your wisdom and partnership is highly valued.

We all appreciate our families more than we can say. We have been blessed with understanding wives and marvelous children. You give us great joy and motivate us to do our best.

Contents

The Critical Yard:

Why Sales Professionals Need to Evolve

"The strength of the relationship breaks all ties in my favor."
—Pete Severns, top sales professional, MotorWerks of Barrington

"I'm just looking."
—Just about every person ever to walk into a shoe store

Sales Failures Teach Us about How to Be Successful

My first sales call was with a regular client of a firm that had just hired me. It was an important sale that I was told would be an easy close, but would require me to meet with the client in person. The most memorable part of this experience was the time required to carry it out. Here is the breakdown:

Driving from Chicago to the client's office in
    Upper Michigan = eight hours
Walking from the parking lot to the client's office = one minute
Introducing myself to the client = twelve minutes
Giving my sales pitch = eight minutes
Listening to the client say no = ten seconds
Recovering from the client saying no = two minutes
Walking to my car = one minute
Driving back to Chicago feeling discouraged = eight hours

The total time my first sales call took was sixteen hours, twenty-four minutes, and ten seconds. And what was supposed to be an easy "yes" turned into a "no."

While driving back to Chicago, I was critiquing myself and realized that I only asked two questions of the client:

1. Can I confirm these Michigan bonds to your account?
2. Where is the men's room?

So what went wrong in the above example? After all of my preparation, travel time, and rehearsal of my pitch, I failed in the most crucial moment of my sales process—the client conversation. The time spent introducing myself, giving my pitch, and receiving the prospect's response took twenty minutes out of my sixteen-and-a-half-hour sales call investment. Those twenty minutes were only a small fraction of the time I invested to make the sale; however, it was the most important part.

I managed that conversation poorly and the results speak for themselves. That experience taught me how important it is to be good while sitting across the table with a client. To be unusually successful as a sales professional, you must master the art of the client/prospect conversation. We refer to that vital client/prospect conversation as the "critical yard."

Those of us who are avid football watchers know about crossing this critical yard in sports. It is fourth down—where there is only one yard to go to the goal line. The coach has to decide if he wants his team to go for the field goal or go for the touchdown. But what is one yard? You wouldn't think that moving the ball one yard should be all that difficult! However, this is a critical yard. The team might have already covered eighty-plus yards to get there, but if they cannot cross that last yard, then their efforts will result in failure. One yard doesn't sound like much, but at that moment, it is crucial.

In sales, that critical yard is the symbolic three feet separating you and your potential client. It is the mysterious distance between you and the prospect that will determine if you are going to make a sale or get nothing for your efforts. Sales professionals are always trying to bridge that critical yard. For some, their attempts to "go for that touchdown" (i.e., getting the sale) end in failure, while others frequently achieve their goals and experience success. Sometimes that yard seems like the entire distance of the football field.

Highly successful sales professionals have mastered crossing that critical yard with ease and habit. Others remain frustrated by their inability to cross that yard as often as they wish they could. We imagine that most of our readers are somewhere between these two groups. This book will give you a structured and disciplined approach for effectively crossing that critical yard.

We believe that the true secret to crossing that critical yard is to shift the conversation from a traditional sales approach to a process that takes the structure of consultative selling (the process of being a consultant to your prospect rather than focusing on selling your product) and combines it with the art of a coaching conversation. While consultative selling has been around for a while and has been adopted by many, what is unique about this book is that we will weave consultative selling with coaching skills and establish a focused and disciplined model for creating dynamic and successful client/prospect conversations. This three-step model creates an interaction and dynamic that will increase your ability to make the sale and will even save you energy and hassles along the way. Developing a style of consultative coaching will help you take your critical yard skills to a new level and dramatically impact your performance and your results.

What Are Top Sales Professionals Saying?

In preparing for this book, we interviewed successful sales professionals from many different industries. What these top sales professionals told us matched our personal research. Today's client has changed and those individuals who continue to be successful in sales are adapting to these changes. We interviewed Pete Severns and his sales manager Tom Martin of MotorWerks of Barrington. Both of these successful individuals focused on the role of the relationship for creating repeat business and a positive experience for their clients. Tom Martin told us how he trains his sales staff to greet prospects. A sample greeting is, "We have several kinds of cars I can show you. However, before I do that, it would help me if I understood how you plan to use it. Would you mind if I begin with a couple of questions?" Tom believes that you cannot serve the client well unless you know what the client truly wants. If you don't listen to your clients, then you are less likely to really match their needs and create a positive buying experience for them. This book will help you develop a structured and discipline approach for maximizing the buyer's experience.

Who Can Use This Book?

There are three levels of sales professionals that differ greatly in their ability to get results—rookies who do not know how to engage prospects and clients; an average group of sales people who create some engagement, but then shift to a monologue; and top sales professionals who know how to effectively engage their prospects in a dialogue and co-create a sale. Obviously, I started my career on the bottom rung of the ladder.

Which are you? Do you have an effective system for aiding prospects and genuinely co-creating a sale in a way that creates little to no resistance and unbreakable client relationships? If you are a true sales professional, then it is your job to understand and adapt to your ever-changing prospect (at least if you want to make a good living). If you are a sales manager, then it is your obligation to have a format against which to train, give feedback to, and mentor your sales staff. If you do not have a highly disciplined and structured approach, then you may be good, but you are not creating the results of which you are capable.

Almost everyone is in sales. It doesn't matter if you are in financial services or real estate or if you are a minister or a lawn keeper. Sales in the form of convincing, persuading, or aiding is part of what all of us do to varying degrees on a daily basis. Some people are absolutely terrible at sales and some are effortless masters. In a world full of sales professionals, it is often the ability to effectively handle that critical yard that separates the winners from the losers (or even the mediocre).

What makes a sales professional successful? Interestingly, what made someone an incredible sales professional in the past is not what makes for a successful sales professional in the twenty-first century (and we will cover this in later chapters). To be effective in sales, you can't follow the curve—you have to stay ahead of it or be part of creating it. Can you imagine the old car salesmen of the past being effective in today's environment? Our world has changed dramatically and sales professionals who refuse to evolve will die off like the dinosaurs of the past. But if you bought this book, then you probably know that new techniques and approaches are essential in this day and age.

For what industries is this book appropriate? Many types of sales professionals can benefit from learning coaching skills for a sales situation. Your authors have a diversity of experience when it comes to their selling background. They have sold in multiple industries and in a variety of positions. Many of the examples in this book are from the financial services industry because the authors' current clientele are weighted heavily in this area. However, given that the authors have nearly one hundred years of combined selling experience, the principles and skills taught in this book can be used in almost any industry, including:

- Financial services
- Coaching and training

- Network marketing
- Automobile industry
- Mortgage industry
- Pharmaceutical sales
- Insurance
- Real estate

Basically, any industry that involves selling to customers could benefit from the principles in this book.

In this book we will teach you a disciplined and structured system of consultative selling processes with the art of coaching to help you:

✓ engage clients quickly and effectively
✓ decrease resistance and rejection
✓ guide clients to self-discover their needs through an energetic dialogue
✓ form a collaborative close with your prospects
✓ get rewarding results from your efforts both financially and personally

If any part of your success depends on your ability to sell, then you must learn how to adapt to the new age of client. You must take your job seriously and dedicate yourself to the science of making the sale. You must understand how to cross the critical yard.

What This Book Is and Is Not

This book is a powerful resource for helping sales professionals develop a disciplined coaching style to create powerful results and deep customer satisfaction. Our focus is exclusively on the conversation with the prospect. Therefore, this book is not about prospecting or getting referrals (except by osmosis, as the coaching approach will automatically create greater referrals from your customers). This is a resource for making the sale itself with a specific focus on the sales conversation. This book is about you transforming to the next level and dramatically improving your ability to cross that critical yard. It is for those of you who do not want to be a "vendor," but rather want to build long-term relationships that you can positively impact.

The Structure of This Book

Each chapter of the resource that you are holding follows the same structure. It flows as follows:

- **Quotes**–Like most sales professionals, we love quotes. Therefore, each chapter will get you in the right mood with either a humorous or meaningful quote related to the chapter topic.
- **Overview**–Gives a summary of what you will find in the chapter.
- **Tales from the Playing Field**–Provides a story from our own or one of our client's experiences related to the challenging profession of sales (some names and unimportant details will be changed to protect confidentiality). To avoid confusion, we use the pronoun "I" when telling our personal stories without regard for which author is "speaking."
- **Principles**–This section discusses the chapter topic in detail, detailing principles, perspectives, and information.

• **Exercises**–The final segment of each section contains questions and exercises that were built to be done alone or in training sessions with others.

We highly encourage you to follow this structure and actually do the exercises. No one masters their craft if they are not willing to put in the time and effort necessary to excel. You have made the first step by purchasing this book. Take the next step by fully utilizing the information and substance found in the following chapters. Now join us as we unite consultative selling and coaching skills to create a disciplined model for making the sale.

Section I

The Case for Coaching

Chapter 1

The Crisis in Sales:

How Titles Are Shifting, but Skills Are Not!

"There are worse things in life than death. Have you ever spent an evening with an insurance salesman?"
—Woody Allen

"You think you hate it now, but wait till you drive it."
—Car salesman from the movie *Vacation*

Overview

At one point they were stockbrokers, then they became financial advisors; next, some became wealth consultants. Financial services is just one of many industries that has embraced the concept of the sales professional as consultant. In this chapter, we will look at how the titles of the sales professional have changed but much of the behavior has not. In addition, we will explore other challenges and trends that are creating obstacles for the sales professional. We will discuss how these trends create subtle and inescapable dangers for the sales professional that can only be addressed by evolving into the next level of sales success. Finally, we will present the need to have a structured and disciplined model to successfully navigate this evolution.

Tales from the Playing Field

I was ready to buy a new car and I knew the exact model I wanted. Being an experienced car buyer (and one who had been burned in the past), I wanted to do my research. Therefore, I bought the right issue of *Client Reports.* I investigated the right websites. I went to CarMax to find out how much they were selling the car for. In other words, I was pretty educated by the time I met John at a different dealership.

John had a slick style and greeted me like we were long lost brothers. He immediately took control of the conversation. As I was listening to his monologue, I started getting impatient. Finally I said, "John, we don't have to go through all of this; I know exactly what I want and how much I want to pay for it." My direct approach seemed to throw John off of his game a little, but we went back to his desk and started our negotiations.

I told John that I didn't want to be "sold" and that I would rather just have an honest and up-front conversation about the car and the details of the deal. I went on to say, "I'll be honest with you, John. I know exactly what you paid for this car and I have a feeling about what would be a fair profit for you, so this is what I am willing to pay." I then quoted my figure. John sat back in his chair and just shook his head. "Oh, your figures are all wrong," he said. "You probably got this by looking on the Internet and they never get these right. In fact, we paid more than this for the car." I looked at John straight in the eyes and told him that we could talk about whether he felt the profit margins were fair, but that given my authentic approach with him, I would not tolerate any of the usual tricks.

He immediately assured me of his honesty and acted offended by my statements, claiming, "I can show you the invoice to prove I would lose money on this deal." At that point, I informed him that I knew that the invoices contained items on them that I considered part of the profit and I would not count these as contributing to their cost. He told me that I was wrong and went back to talk with his manager. When he returned, he showed me the invoice and tried some distraction techniques. As I suspected, the invoice proved that he had lied to me and I walked out. Of course, he then chased me to offer the car again at the price that I originally quoted, joking that his manager made him take his previous approach with me. However, by then it was too late; he had broken my trust.

What John didn't know is that I was fine with paying him more money than my initial offer. I've been on commission my entire professional life. I know what it is like to struggle financially and I know what it is like to do well. If he had been honest with me and said that he just wanted to make more profit, I would have bumped my offer up significantly to get the car. I'm fine with a skilled sales professional earning what he is worth. What I was not fine with was someone treating me like I was ignorant of the facts. I was too educated of a client to fall for his tricks, so he lost the sale. And I am not alone. Clients today are different from clients of the past.

The Fine Line between Sale and No Sale

The number of savvy clients is dramatically increasing. Clients know how to research using the Internet and other sources of information to help determine what is and is not a good deal. They are more educated and capable than ever before, and have the world at their typing fingers. While this is fantastic for the client, it can represent a huge challenge for the traditional sales professional.

With greater education and knowledge comes shifting demands. Clients want more respect from those trying to sell products and services, and don't want to "feel" sold on anything. You cannot treat the client of today like the client of yesterday. They are as different as night and day. The figure below demonstrates the relationship between the sophistication of the client and the skill level needed to be successful in sales. This, of course, is common sense, but surprisingly, many do not put this into practice.

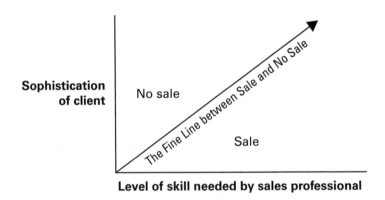

Level of skill needed by sales professional

This shift has created a huge challenge to the traditional sales professional—it is just plain harder to sell to people. That is, it is harder only if you are still using traditional techniques. Those using traditional techniques come home drained at the end of the day. Some are extremely hard workers but are wasting their energy using approaches and tactics that are transparent and offensive to some. Even those sales professionals with noble intentions (and we believe this describes most) can finish their workweek completely de-energized and fatigued if they are using the wrong approach.

Burnout is a common phenomenon for those in sales. We believe this occurs because of the lack of long-term fuel for success. The sales professional who is out constantly trying to convince others, handling objections, and attempting multiple trial closes will deplete herself of energy if she does not learn to recharge and replenish her power source (that is why we cover the energy of confidence in chapter 6). In addition, the true worth today is to genuinely add value to the clients' lives. Those sales professionals that add real value will excel in today's environment.

The True Purpose of Making a Sale

Lousy and unethical sales professionals have given the career of sales a bad name. However, sales can be an honorable calling and should be treated with respect, accountability, and a true spirit of service.

Selling is basically about having the skills to make people happy. You can make them happy by introducing them to a product that makes their lives easier and more enjoyable, or you can please them by providing a valuable service to them. Either way, the successful sales professional's main role is really about adding value to the buyers' lives by making them content.

But we forget this sometimes. Because sales can be financially rewarding, we can lose sight of the deeper meaning and purpose. Don't get us wrong—we like making a good living. We like providing well for our families and we like being able to aid those with lesser means. However, to benefit from this book, it can't just be about the money for you. Oh sure, we firmly believe from experiences with our clients the fact that the money does come. But it comes from a genuine desire to please your clients and having the skills to do that in an authentic and powerful way.

In the past, sales professionals could "fake" their level of care to a certain degree. Today, the prospect is much more skeptical and can "sniff" out those who are just going through the mechanics of the sales process in order to benefit themselves.

Clients Are Wise to Manipulative Techniques

Along with true care and genuineness, we also need to be highly skilled sales professionals (today more than ever). People are harder to reach. They screen out sales professionals through email and voicemail. They are wise to the tricks that traditional salespeople try to pull. How many of us roll our eyes when the person trying to sell us a car claims that she has to go back to talk to her sales manager to get some figures? How many of us buy in to the telemarketer who says that we have earned the right to a special service from one of our credit card company's strategic partners? How many people believe the network marketer who claims that we will be making six figures in six months if we just "work the plan"?

We are now a nation of doubters. We see the old style of sales as "tricky" and can't stand it when someone pretends to listen only to "mount the attack" soon afterwards by providing us with a product or solution that has nothing to do with what we said. We have been burned and we won't be fooled again.

The Internet, client reports, and other sources of information are readily available. If we want to buy a digital camera, we can compare twenty brands immediately online for features and benefits. We no longer have to trust the word of the sales representative–and in fact, most of the time we wouldn't even think about trusting their words. We don't trust our government. We don't trust our employers. Sometimes we don't even trust our spouse. Why in the world should we trust someone who is trying to sell us something?

Sales professionals have tried to adapt to this trend by creating the image of being consultants. Intuitively they know that people want a consultation rather than a sales pitch. They know that people are looking for a sales professional who understands their needs and can coach them to the right decision. However, the main approach to accomplishing this shift in identity seems to be printing new business cards.

What People Are Putting on Their Business Cards

Have you noticed how many people in sales today are "consultants"? We did a quick Internet search and here are some of the first "consultants" that appeared:

- Veterinary Consultant
- SAP Consultant
- Restaurant Consultant
- Maintenance Management Consultant
- Help-Desk Consultant
- Business Consultant
- Sport Consultant

- Financial Consultant
- Insurance Consultant
- Mathematics Consultant
- Car Consultant

It is obvious that titles are changing. People in sales have discovered that people would rather have a consultant than be sold to. How wonderful for the client, right? Sales professionals are becoming consultants! You would think that the clients would be ecstatic. Unfortunately, for many the transformation only goes as far as getting new business cards printed up. Putting "consultant" on your business card only means that you are a traditional sales professional with nice, shiny new cards.

The fact is that while titles are changing, for many, skills and mindsets are not. This results in a garbage in/garbage out interaction between sales professional and client. If you do not have the appropriate focus and skill set to ask powerful questions, listen deeply, and reflect accurately, you are unlikely to "consult" well and truly provide your client with the best solution. Think about your business card. What does it say about who you are? How well do you live up to that advertising? In other words, do your skills live up to the promotion on your business card? If they don't, then you are creating a problem for yourself.

From Success to Significance

There is one last factor that is causing a crisis for sales professionals (many of whom are also baby boomers). This factor is related to midlife. There is an interesting developmental milestone that occurs for many people in their forties (it can, of course, occur earlier or later—it is just more common when you pass forty years old). This milestone is the shift from focusing on success to the desire for significance. Once someone has experienced a high level of success for some period of time, she realizes that while fun, it just isn't enough. She realizes that there is more to life, and starts developing strong desires to leave some sort of legacy behind. Many of those who see themselves as traditional sales professionals feel unfulfilled by their profession. "Isn't there any more to life than convincing someone to buy this stupid product?" might cross their minds more than once or twice. Even those that have been highly financially rewarded for their efforts start questioning the eventual emptiness that comes with success. This is when many people want to find another way of impacting the world and people's lives.

The wonderful thing is that you can find great significance in a sales position with the right skills, mindset, and results. Those who successfully transition through this phase of life discover that the position/job has less to do with creating significance than *how* you do the position or job. The three-step coaching model provided in this book will help you find greater significance in a sales position and have a significant impact on the lives of your clients and yourself.

Why Transform in Your Sales Skills and Approach?

So why should you care about transforming into the next level of sales professional? To summarize:

✓ Clients are more educated and demanding, and the sales professional of the past is as antiquated as the dinosaur.

✓ The traditional style of sales takes too much time and energy, resulting in prospect resistance and lesser results.

✓ The traditional style of sales falls short in fulfilling the noble calling of sales, which is adding true value to your client's life.

✓ Clients are smarter than ever before and turned off by manipulative techniques and approaches.

✓ If you call yourself (verbally or on your business card) a consultant and act like a traditional salesperson, then you are setting yourself up to fail the expectations that you have just created for your prospect.

✓ A different style of sales can help sales professionals who want greater impact and significance in their lives.

The true sales professional does not need us to convince them of the need to grow. They know it and they do it. So from this point out, we are assuming that you are that sales professional. Given you recognize the crisis that we are discussing, we offer an approach that will deal with each of the above issues effectively and in a way that increases your impact and financial rewards. As we have stated, we believe that the solution to this crisis is for the sales professional to move from the identity of the traditional sales professional or sales consultant to a deeper identity of a coach.

Can You Be 1 Percent Better?

The top people in any field tend not to be 50 percent better than the lesser (but good) performers. Often, they are only 1 or 2 percent better. Successful athletes such as Tiger Woods are not 50 percent better than their peers. When you analyze their scores, there is often only a small percentage of difference in results. But what an impact that 1 percent can have! It can make the difference between winning a million dollars and winning $100,000. So even if you are reading this and thinking that you are pretty good at consultative selling, we want to challenge you to look for that 1 or 2 percent in this book that will take your selling skills to that next level. We propose you do this by learning to master how to *coach* the sale. As you explore the rest of this book, you will see how a coaching approach takes the best of consultative selling and makes it even more powerful, respectful, and effective. Coaching the sale will help you cross that critical yard, build unbreakable client relationships, and truly aid people in their lives in the process. Part of the effectiveness of the coaching model is based on the power of self-discovery.

The Heart and Soul of Coaching

For those readers who have children, you know that you can instruct your children until you are blue in the face, but the real change in behavior will come when they realize the lesson for themselves. You wish that they would listen to you, and sometimes they do. However, many times the most powerful lesson is when they discover the truth on their own. Interestingly, it is not that different for adults. The power of self-discovery stays with us our entire lives. We have natural defenses that pop up when someone is trying to convince us of something. Especially today, with all of the scandals and behind-the-scenes revelations, we just don't trust as much as we use to. Those of us who are over forty remember what it was like to not have to worry about locking your doors at night and how picking up hitchhikers was no big deal. Today, people are more educated and more suspicious of promises. They have heard tales of or have experienced unethical sales professionals who have taken advantage of people. Therefore, attempts to *convince* them of the value of your product or service are often met with disbelief, negativity, and resistance. However, if they self-discover the value of your product or service, then they are interested, engaged, and open. Self-discovery is the heart and soul of coaching.

One of the reasons I love living in Chicago is the great Lake Michigan. I love to boat, and several years ago, I made a decision to get a different vessel. After doing my research, I had my choices narrowed down to two boats. So I went to the Chicago Boat Show and went over to see the first of the two crafts I was considering.

The salesperson's name was Ron, and after a brief greeting, he led me to the back of the boat and suggested we start by looking at the engines. Now, the engine was not my biggest point of interest, but I agreed. Down in the engine compartment, Ron detailed for me the wonders of two Caterpillar diesel 420HP engines and the turbo charger performance. He also went over the trim tabs systems and integrated hydraulics of the engine compartment. Ron was so excited that he failed to notice my discomfort in being in such a small space. After what seemed like an hour, I finally convinced Ron to let me out and see the rest of the boat.

Upon completing my tour of the boat, I went over to see the second boat. As I approached the sales professional, Rich looked up and asked if I was interested in the boat. As

I nodded, he asked, "Before you get on, do you mind if I ask you a few questions?" I said, "Sure," thinking that as long as we don't have to go into the engine compartment I would be fine. Rich went on to ask how I planned to use the boat. I replied that I would be using it on the weekends to vacation in Grand Haven, Michigan. He went on to ask me who would drive this boat. I told him I would want my wife and two oldest sons to be able to drive it in case I was unable to drive for any reason.

With that he asked, "How many kids do you have?" I replied, "Six," which somewhat stunned him (as it does many people). After thinking for a moment, he asked, "Would you mind if I show you the number one reason why people with children buy this boat?" With that, we went down a five-step stairway into the galley, and went to the back of the boat to a small bedroom with two twin size beds and a TV in the corner.

Once in this small room, he pointed to the TV and communicated that this setup was the number one reason why people buy this boat. Very confused, I asked, "Because of the little black and white TV?" "Yes," he replied. "You see, no boat is big enough for kids, let alone six of them. After thirty to forty-five minutes in any cruise you have taken, what are your kids doing?" I replied that they are getting antsy and are bothering their mother for something to do. "What people do when this happens," Rich said, "is they get a *Lion King* or *Mission Impossible* tape, take it below and file the kids in, shut the door, and there you have two hours of peace and quiet. Put on some coffee, music, or whatever."

He then looked me right in the eyes and said, "Do you think this might help make your wife's boating experience more pleasurable?" I immediately began thinking that really would be helpful since she has very little peace and quiet. Without missing a beat, he asked if my wife was ever concerned about safety issues, especially with the little ones. "Of course," I answered. Rich proceeded to take me to the top of the boat where he showed me a walkway the manufacturer had placed there in the middle of the boat so the kids wouldn't have to go on the outside of the boat on a narrow platform to get from the back to the front of the boat. He then asked, "Do you think this center walk might help alleviate any safety concerns you and your wife might have about the kids?"

Rich was a smart man. There was now something going on inside of me. All I focused on was a peaceful and safer boat ride for my family and a more pleasurable boating experience.

So guess which boat I bought? Yes, it was the second boat. But the real story here is that before I interacted with these two salespeople, I was 100 percent sure I would buy the first boat. I had loved this boat and wanted that exact model for years. However, Rich literally stole me away from the first salesperson because of one simple concept–he understood, believed in, and trusted the power of questions and how they can turn a monologue into a dialogue and uncover big pieces of information. Rich knew the value of self-discovery and how to coach the sale.

The beauty of the above story is that the experience of buying a boat was not just a sales transaction. Rather, the person selling me the boat helped me create a vision of how that boat was going to make my life better. He helped guide me to a great buying decision for my family in an effortless and easy manner. He helped me self-discover that this purchase was going to make my life better. He coached me to a great decision. While his style seemed flexible and flowing, I have no doubt that he knew what he was doing and was following a disciplined approach for making the sale.

By the way, Rich was one of the top sales professionals in his boat line for five years running. So ask yourself: does it really pay to ask questions? Just ask Rich.

We work with lots of professionals and we know that self-discovery can be a difficult concept for some traditional sales professionals to buy into. Common barriers are thoughts like:

- I don't have time for them to self-discover.
- I lead the discovery, not them.
- This is all just silly psychobabble.
- Prospects just want to be educated.

And yet, at the same time, they know that something is shifting and that selling to clients is more challenging now than ever. The mind is a difficult thing to change and can become very set in its thinking patterns. Progressive sales professionals have to have a complete mind *shift* when it comes to coaching the sale. The figure below demonstrates to what we are referring:

	Old mind*set*	Needed mind *shift*
The sales professional's most powerful tool	Product knowledge	Client connection
Goal of meeting	Making the sale	Meeting the need
Role of the sales professional	Giving solutions	Co-creating solutions with prospect
Approach to prospect	Get information, then give an answer that meets a need	Guide the prospect to discover the needs and solutions
Greatest skill of the sales professional	Persuasion	Asking powerful questions
Role of advice	Crucial	Minimal
Role of energy	Energy of sales professional drives the conversation, equaling energy expenditures	Conversation creates energy for both the sales professional and the prospect
How to close the sale	Have prepared responses to any objections and ask for the sale	Follow the coaching conversation and then ask the prospect his or her perspective and desires

Now, we are not saying that all of the elements under the old mindset are bad. (In fact, some of them can still exist in our coaching model.) We are only presenting that they need to evolve to the next level. The old mindsets are not necessarily negative; they just need to shift to something even more positive and impacting.

We once ran an experiment and timed individuals who used the old way of selling in a phone selling situation. The participants averaged seventeen minutes of airtime for calls pitching their products and showed no ability to close. After training them on this model, the average airtime was seven and a half minutes and each call ended with agreements and next steps. Once you learn this model, it saves you both time and effort, and leads to results.

We hope that we have convinced you of the importance of being 1 percent better than the next sales professional and challenging your old ways of thinking. In the following exercises, we will help you explore your personal concepts, viewpoints, and past experiences of coaching. By bringing up memories of your previous interactions with a coach, we hope to reignite the passion that comes from working with a great coach. Then in the next chapter, we will help you combine consultative selling and coaching to create a sales style that will excel with today's clients and prospects.

EXERCISE: Your Best Coach

Describe your best coach ever. Your example can be from business, sports, home, or other sources. Write down a few sentences about the coach and then list ten qualities your coach had or ten things you appreciated about him or her—in other words, ten things that made the person a great coach.

My best coach was

_____

_____

Words or phrases that described my coach are:

_____

_____

_____

_____

_____

_____

_____

_____

Ten things that made this person a great coach are:

1. _____

2. _____

3. _____

4. _____

5. _____

6. _____

7. _____

8. _____

9. _____

10. _____

EXERCISE: Comparing Your Coach

The following represents a list of common phrases or words used to describe effective coaches. Using the list below, rate your coach on a scale of one to five in terms of how well he or she demonstrated the following qualities.

Respectful

1	2	3	4	5
Not at all	Mildly describes	Neutral	Strongly describes	Perfectly

Listened to me

1	2	3	4	5
Not at all	Mildly describes	Neutral	Strongly describes	Perfectly

Knew my goals

1	2	3	4	5
Not at all	Mildly describes	Neutral	Strongly describes	Perfectly

Guided me to my answers

1	2	3	4	5
Not at all	Mildly describes	Neutral	Strongly describes	Perfectly

Empowered me

1	2	3	4	5
Not at all	Mildly describes	Neutral	Strongly describes	Perfectly

Cared about me

1	2	3	4	5
Not at all	Mildly describes	Neutral	Strongly describes	Perfectly

Had confidence in me

1	2	3	4	5
Not at all	Mildly describes	Neutral	Strongly describes	Perfectly

Challenged me to do more

1	2	3	4	5
Not at all	Mildly describes	Neutral	Strongly describes	Perfectly

Inspired me

1	2	3	4	5
Not at all	Mildly describes	Neutral	Strongly describes	Perfectly

Talked things out with me

1	2	3	4	5
Not at all	Mildly describes	Neutral	Strongly describes	Perfectly

Reflect on which of these characteristics you want to show as a sales professional.

Chapter 2

A Structured and Disciplined Approach to Sales:

Uniting Consultative Selling and Coaching

"I always take the time to find out who a customer is before I ask what they want."
—Tom Martin, sales manager, MotorWerks of Barrington

"Bad habits are like a comfortable bed: easy to get into, but hard to get out of."
—Anonymous

Overview

There is no doubt that, as of the time of this writing, "coaching" is hot. However, many people are using this term differently. In this chapter, we will explore both consultative selling and coaching and make a case for uniting the two. We will introduce a model that is simple, flexible, and effective, which can be used to increase your own selling ability or the selling ability of those you manage. By uniting consultative selling approaches with the philosophy, skills, and dialogue nature of coaching, we will demonstrate a model that can help any individual or organization take their sales to the next level. However, first we will make the case for learning a structured and disciplined model.

Tales from the Playing Field

I was in San Francisco experiencing one of those common two-hour delays when I struck up a conversation with our pilot who was also waiting. He had been flying for decades and seemed extremely knowledgeable. I asked him, "What do you do in the cockpit when you take off?" His answer was very profound. He stated, "I do the same thing every single time." He then went on to explain that there were about fifty things he needed to do before taking off to ensure a safe flight. In addition, he emphasized that there were about twenty-seven things he needed to do every time he shut down the plane. He talked about following the same sequence and structure every time. I asked him, "As experienced as you are, you still need to follow the same sequence every time?" to which he replied, "Absolutely–I never deviate. I do it exactly the same way every time I get in that plane." Of course, as I thought about it, this made perfect sense. In fact, I was very pleased that he wasn't just jumping in the cockpit and figuring out what he needed to do at that time.

Unfortunately, unlike this pilot, many sales professionals work by instinct or by "winging it." In this chapter, we will explore combining consultative selling and coaching to create a *structured and disciplined approach* that will serve you well to connect with and sell to today's clients. Let's start with looking at the evolution of consultative selling.

What Is Consultative Selling?

Growth came to the field of sales years ago in the form of consultative selling. This was an important shift because consultative selling started the process of focusing less on the initial pitch and more on trying to understand your prospect's needs and wants. In its pure form (which seems rarely practiced), consultative selling took the sophistication of the sales process up a notch. It required the sales professional to work at understanding his or her client's real needs before trying to make the pitch.

Traditional selling techniques were primarily based on information and persuasion. You were taught how to build rapport, how to handle objections, and how to close the sale. Sales training often focused exclusively on how to get the customer to buy your product and rarely questioned whether your product was truly the best for the client. When consultative selling was introduced, sales professionals began focusing on how to:

- discover needs
- match product benefits to client needs
- strive for a long-term relationship
- develop powerful networks

Many sales professionals see the consultative selling process as an approach that is more respectful to the customer. After all, at least with this process, you are attempting to find out if the customer really needs your product and why.

However, many sales professionals with only average skills have taken this process and subverted its respectful intent. For the client, the initial consultation can feel more like an interrogation than a discussion. This conversation is usually under the control of the sales professional and still can appear manipulative and selfish. Some sales professionals who are mediocre in the consultative selling process are transparent to their prospects. The potential customer can see that the sales professional is quickly and mechanically moving through a series of questions with obvious anticipation to get to his or her pitch. Once they quickly draw out the prospect's information, the "conversation" becomes one sided and the big monologue occurs. Again, this has worked decently in the past, but today it is a recipe for disaster.

We believe that the consultative selling process needs to be adjusted in order to evolve to the next level of sophistication, effectiveness, and respect. There is a critical yard that many sales professionals are not crossing. They work their tails off prospecting customers, but they often fumble the ball when it comes to crossing that last yard. The good news is that transforming to the next level does not have to be as complex as some believe. By adding coaching skills to the consultative selling process, sales professionals can cross the critical yard with ease and effectiveness.

What Is a Coach?

It is interesting hearing different ideas of what a coach is and is not. In one workshop that we did for one of the major financial wire houses, we had planned a series of exercises around the concept of coaching. The first activity we introduced was for participants to choose one of two nametags that came in their welcome pack. One nametag said "Financial Advisor." The other nametag said "Wealth Coach." We told the participants that they could choose whichever of the two nametags they wanted to represent their identity in financial services. We fully expected the vast majority of them to pick the nametag of Wealth Coach.

Surprisingly, the room was split about 50/50. What was most interesting, though, was the reasons that the 50 percent chose *not* to wear the Wealth Coach nametag. As we asked for feedback, here are a few of the things we heard:

- "A coach bosses people around and that's not me."
- "A coach gets in his players' faces; I can't do that with my clients."
- "A coach just gives motivational speeches, and I have more skills than that."
- "I act as more of a guide for my clients than someone bossing them around."

We were shocked. The very reasons they were choosing not to call themselves coaches were the reasons we do call ourselves coaches. In other words, we don't believe great coaches boss people around or get in your face or just give motivational speeches. Oh sure, you hear stories of the coaches of yesteryear who did this, but that was a different time and place. While there are still some highly aggressive coaches out there, you will find more Phil Jackson types being successful in today's environment than the Bobby Knight types.

We were able to break participants free of this thinking by simply asking them to pair up and talk about the best coach they ever had (just like we had you do in the last chapter). When they had finished and we got the group back together, we pulled these qualities out of the group. When the group was focused on their best coach they share qualities like:

- Believed in me
- Knew I could do more than I ever knew
- Really took the time to know me

- Challenged me to do the right thing
- Listened to me
- Respected me
- Built my confidence
- Inspired me

It was interesting to watch the room shift as they talked about their best coach. You could feel the positive energy in the room and laughter and smiles became much more spontaneous. The group dynamics recharged as they started remembering the huge impact that their best coach had on their lives.

A Definition of Coaching in Sales

Here is how we define coaching in a sales situation:

A coaching approach to sales involves a relationship between a sales professional and an interested individual, which creates an environment of respect, safety, challenge, and accountability. This relationship motivates all involved to find the best solutions possible and co-create successful and profitable results whenever possible, for both the sales professional and prospect. These successful results will often impact both positively in business and in life.

Does that sound silly to you? Or can you believe that the sales process could capture that noble a purpose? At the core of this definition is a true interest in what serves the prospect well in business. The impact on the prospect's life is also included for a very specific reason. That reason is that when you impact both the life and the business success of a prospect, then they become clients for life.

A common chart in the field of coaching and consulting is presented below. You are asked to consider whether someone is a help in your business, your life, or both, and to put a check mark in the right box.

	Help in life—**No**	Help in life—**Yes**
Help in business—**No**		
Help in business—**Yes**		

If you wish to do so, you can fill in the boxes as follows as it applies to a selling relationship:

- When I do not help you in business and I do not help you in life, then we have *no relationship*.
- When I help you in life but I do not help you in business, then our relationship is likely a *friendship*.
- When I help you in business but I have no impact on your life, then I am a *vendor* to you.
- When I help you in business and I help you in life, then I become a *trusted coach*.

In other words, if I sell you a product that works well, then you might trust me as a great vendor. When I sell you a product that helps you reach your goals, become more profitable, advance in your profession, and improve your life, then I have become a valued and trusted coach. So ask yourself, "Do I want to be a vendor, or do I want to be a trusted coach?" It is up to you!

Core Beliefs in a General Coaching Model

At its core, coaching is about how you *view* your prospect. The level of respect and belief in your prospect and people in general is crucial for truly adopting a coaching philosophy to the sales process. Below is a list of common coaching philosophies found in most coach training programs. Coaches believe that:

• The person being coached is creative and capable
• There is greater motivation when the coach connects with the client's agenda
• A coaching relationship requires mutual respect, trust, and honesty
• A coach aids a client in overcoming obstacles to success
• They help clients be accountable and move to action

Now apply those same principles to a sales situation:

• The prospect is creative and capable of making the best buying decision.
• There is greater motivation when the sales professional connects with the prospect's agenda.
• A solid sales relationship requires a high level of trust.
• Sales professionals aid prospect in overcoming obstacles to success.
• Sales professionals help prospects be accountable and move to action.

Are these really so hard to believe in a sales situation? And if you believe them, are these philosophies really that difficult to put into practice? If you are doubtful that this will result in greater sales–great! That means you are really thinking this through instead of just accepting our opinion. Those are the kind of readers we want! That fits perfectly with a coaching model. You will change to a coaching style in your sales when it makes sense to *you*! While we will act as guides, you must self-discover the impact of a coaching style to fully embrace this style.

A talented coach:

- understands the client's goals and motivators
- asks powerful questions
- listens well
- reflects and clarifies
- strategizes and problem solves
- works through blocks to achieving goals
- moves conversation to action/solution

We feel that these are the same skill sets and shifts required to create a powerful and motivating sales situation, and we will look at each of these skills in more detail in the next three chapters.

Give—Get/Give—Guide

By uniting the structure of consultative selling and the philosophy and skills of coaching, you can have an incredible model to aid clients and increase your sales. Let's make a final distinction between traditional sales, consultative selling, and coaching the sale by using the words give, get/give, and guide.

Give

In many old-fashioned, traditional sales models, the main focus is on *giving* information to the client. The theory is if you give the client enough information and do it persuasively enough, then you will make your sale. In this approach, the sales professional tends to do most of the talking with a heavy emphasis on traditional sales stages. As a traditional sales professional, knowledge and persuasion are your most powerful tools. At the extreme, traditional sales, or give, is like a tour guide coming to you and telling you where you should go on vacation and why. They would do this without ever checking with whether you like exotic places, Europe, or the Midwest.

Get/Give

The evolution from traditional sales to consultative selling was a welcomed one. In the consultative sales model, you theoretically take the time to *get* information from the prospect before *giving* your solution to the prospect's need. Of course, many have perverted this process where they ask a few simple questions and then merely dive back into the traditional sales monologue of giving information and trying to persuade the prospect. The purpose of a consultative selling process was noble—really knowing your client's needs and wants and matching them up to the right solutions. However, the execution of the consultative selling process has left much to be desired. Listening well, analyzing, and matching solutions to goals are your most powerful tools as someone who does consultative selling.

Consultative selling, or *get/give* (especially in how it is practiced even more than it is in theory), is like the tour guide asking you briefly where you want to go and then trying to sell you on a trip that may or may not be what you requested, but will be made to fit your request in some way. Imagine him sitting across the table from you as he does this. Then once you buy the adventure, he starts out the door and waves for you to follow. He rarely looks back, but is now determined to lead you on this adventure that he "wisely chose" to match your needs.

Guide

Clients have become aware of this get/give formula and tend to be suspicious of it. They refuse to be "suckered in" by any of the old manipulative techniques. They have been in too many situations where sales professionals have distorted the technique in an artificial and disingenuous way. This prompted us to explore the transformation of the consultative model to help achieve its original and noble goals. This is why we have spent the time and energy to transform consultative selling by uniting it with the coaching model. In our view, coaching skills turn consultative selling into a consistent dialogue. Consultative selling is the structure beneath the dialogue. It is like the chassis of your car. The chassis is crucial for making the car run, but people don't buy the car for the chassis. They buy the whole package. Coaching philosophies, techniques, and approaches integrated with the foundation of consultative selling is a package that people will buy and will benefit from buying. In the process, the sales professional never deviates from the dialogue. In other words, it stays a conversation the entire model rather than being a conversation that converts to a pitch. The client works with you to form a collaborative close and thus co-creates the sale. Thus, in the coaching model, the emphasis is on *guiding* the prospect to the right buying decision.

But what is the role of a really good guide? If you have a personal tour guide, she will take the time to find out what really interests you, she will not allow you to get lost, and she will make sure you enjoy the journey. If you have a guide leading you up a mountain, he will find out about your goals, physical condition, past injuries, and lots of other issues before starting the journey. Once the journey starts, he will be in constant communication with you, checking on your condition and your perspectives as well as, at times, challenging you to keep climbing. He has his eye on the destination of the journey, but never loses sight of you. He adapts the climb to your health, goals, and responses. You *must* be able to trust your guide. Would you let someone you did not trust lead you up Mount Kilimanjaro? Of course not; you must believe that your guide is experienced, understands you, and will not abandon you on any part of the journey. The most powerful tools for the person who coaches the sale are powerful questions, superior communication skills, unshakable confidence, and the ability to guide someone to their own answers.

Coaching the sale corresponds to the term guide. It is like sitting down with a tour guide who truly cares about your likes, dislikes, and goals. If what he has to offer does not fit you, he will not force it. If he starts talking about a certain type of trip and you seem hesitant, he backs off and comes back to trying to understand what you really want. Imagine you and him sitting on the same side of the desk and problem-solving your trip together before you head out on the adventure. Then once you are on the adventure, he is not done with his job, but rather continues to assess if the direction you are taking is right for you.

The Impact of a Coaching Approach on Retention and Referrals

Coaching the sale or guiding the process can have powerful results on client retention and referrals. Early in my career, I met with several people for help with financial planning and investments. One individual with whom I had just started working was advising me on putting some money in an aggressive stock. I was pretty convinced that I wanted to do it and was asking his advice. He stopped the conversation and asked if we could talk more generally for a bit. He then took the time to find out my entire financial picture, my goals, and what kind of security or backup I had financially. Well, it was early enough in my career that I had very little backup. At that point, he advised me to take the money that I was going to put in this aggressive stock and put it in a savings account. He told me that any money above a savings account that reflected three months of my salary should be used with these kinds of investments.

Whether you agree or disagree with his advice is irrelevant to this point. The point is that he could have easily sold me on a product that made him a commission; instead, he was willing to forgo that commission in order to do the right thing for me at that time. Was this a stupid decision on his part? I don't think so. Because of his actions, I have stayed with him for over a decade, I have referred over fifty people to him, and I have purchased many financial products through him. He guided me well, and that bought my loyalty and made me a raving advocate for him.

We hope that you are of the same mindset and can see the critical differences between these types of interactions.

However, agreeing to the concept is only half of the battle. The other half is putting concepts into a method or process that will be successful.

The Case for a Structured and Disciplined Approach

Professionals who have been doing sales for a while sometimes forget what it is like to be starting out. Experienced sales professionals usually have a process (even it they do not realize it) that they follow. The new salesperson does not have the benefit of experience to have this developed process and can feel quite lost at times.

New salespeople who start out without a structured approach often have no idea how to do their job. They ask common questions like:

- "How do I start a call?"
- "Where do I take it once I start?"
- "How do I end the sales call?"

Interestingly, even experienced sales professionals are revisiting these questions due to the fact that sales have become more complex in the twenty-first century and they realize that they will be less successful by using their old process or by trying to "wing it" in the new environment. Think back to our initial story about the airplane pilot. His job was to fly that plane and he would never think about doing it without a disciplined system to ensure that he would safely get himself and his passengers to their destination. These big planes don't fly themselves. They need a skilled professional doing the job that he or she is supposed to do.

Or take golfers: if you are watching a golf tournament on the weekend, have you ever noticed the routines they go through? Have you watched the way they stand behind the ball and just look at it? Then they anticipate the flight and do their little waggle. They line up their feet and their hands and only when everything is right do they take the swing. They don't just do this once. They do it *every single time.* The same ritual occurs with physicians prepping for surgery. Those professionals who treat their jobs seriously and aim to excel have a disciplined process that they follow. The process is not mechanical, but it is disciplined.

So that brings us to the sales professional. Amazingly, many individuals in sales do not have such a process, or do not practice it. Do you have a systematized approach for handling the new client? Do you follow a similar process every time you are in front of a prospect? If not, do you really feel like you are doing as well as you could in making the sale? Top salespeople are disciplined and structured and will not risk their level of success by entering a sales situation without a method.

The Role of the Sales Manager

Sales managers can create powerful results by training their sales force on a system.

Even sales managers often do not use a system to mentor their sales staff. How can you manage others effectively in sales without a system? When I worked for Procter & Gamble early in my career, we had twelve steps that we were supposed to follow on a sales call. After every call, my manager would drill me on these twelve steps. Consequently, I remember

continued

them even to this day. Part of my success at that time was my manager taking the time to help me learn a system that at that time was very effective. A structured system allows a manager or an individual to evaluate a sales call and make improvements to sales skills. Was the sales professional concise enough? Was he specific enough in his recommendations? Did he ask the right questions to fully understand the prospect's needs and buying motivations? Without a system to compare behavior against, it is hard to know what skills need mentoring or improvement. If you are a manager, then we strongly urge you to teach this model to your sales staff and then hold them accountable for executing the model. If you are a sales professional, we strongly encourage you to share this book with your sales manager and ask for the gift of that accountability. Practice the model with your peers or manager to master it.

The Process Must Be Simple

Along with needing a sales process that is structured, we also need a process that is simple. A simple process helps you remember the steps in the heat of the moment. One of our pet peeves is sales training that involves complex models that no one could possibly remember during a sales discussion. Some have thirteen steps to close a prospect, require you to understand sixteen different personalities, or have twenty steps to prepare for the call. It is just too much. We all know that a high-potential sales discussion can be highly pressured and emotional. You need a simple model in these moments to withstand the pressure of the client or prospect interview. You must have a system that is simple enough to remember, but powerful enough to help you get results.

Do you have a system that you follow to ensure your success? If you don't, use the system in this book. If you have a system, does it meet the following criteria?

- Is it structured enough to allow you to constantly improve by comparing your performance to the model?
- Is it simple enough to remember and execute?
- Does it address the changes in the twenty-first-century client?
- Does it get the results of which you know you are capable?

If not, then consider the three-step model that we are presenting in this book.

A Simple Coaching Model Specific to the Sales Interaction

While many parts of a coaching model translate well to sales, it is necessary to tweak the model somewhat in order to make a sale. In pure coaching, the coach does not have an agenda such as making a sale. In a sales situation, there is no way to completely avoid having an agenda. Heck, you have to make a living! However, instead of having an agenda of *making the sale*, advocate the agenda of skillfully *guiding the prospect to make his or her best buying decision.* We believe that sales and loyalty will naturally come when you take this approach.

We also wanted to simplify the model. You don't need to memorize twenty different steps with several different skills to implement a coaching sales model. The sales coaching model that we have developed comes down to three basic steps that we refer to as the 3D model of coaching. These 3 Ds are:

In the "discover" phase of the coaching conversation, you gather the motivations, needs, and perspectives of the prospect. In the "discuss" phase of the coaching conversation, you talk about the different challenges and possible solutions. In the "decide" phase of the coaching conversation, you co-create the outcome of the discussion and move to action. Each phase of the 3D model is distinct and flows clearly into the next stage. Part of the power of the model is that if you get poor sales results from it, you change what you are doing. You can quickly determine whether the product or service just isn't right for the prospect or if you failed to skillfully execute part of the model. If you "messed up," then you simply return to the previous stage of the model to recover and achieve a more successful conversation. Our next three chapters will cover each of the three phases of the 3D sales coaching conversation in detail.

EXERCISE: Sales Style Assessment

Take the following informal assessment to determine your natural sales style. Try to answer the questions as honestly as possible rather than just putting down the "right" answers (faking results on a self-survey test does not really serve you well). This is an up-front survey with no attempt to trick you with the results, so when answering the questions, focus on your *actual behaviors* more than what you *know* is the right way to do it. Also, think about the behaviors you do most often. For each statement, rank the answers. Put a 3 for the answer that best represents your opinion, a 2 for the next matching answer, and a 1 for the answer that least represents your opinion: For now, ignore the letters next to the space in which you put your rating. We will use those later for scoring.

1. I can best tell that I am going to get a sale by:

The quality of my presentation _____ (A)

The quality of the information I have gotten from the prospect _____ (B)

The quality of the relationship with my prospect _____ (C)

2. Effective sales professionals:

Present well _____ (A)

Gather information well _____ (B)

Relate well _____ (C)

3. The best sale I ever made came from:

Knowing my material   _____ (A)

Knowing my prospect's goals   _____ (B)

Knowing my prospect's vision   _____ (C)

4. I can tell if a client is going to buy from me when:

I handle their objections well   _____ (A)

When I match my product to
their need   _____ (B)

When our conversation feels like
a partnership   _____ (C)

**5. In terms of advising a client that my service
or product was not best for him, I:**

Have never done this   _____ (A)

Have rarely done this   _____ (B)

Have done this many times   _____ (C)

6. The best sales professional I know of:

Is an expert in his or her product   _____ (A)

Is an expert in asking the
right questions   _____ (B)

Is an expert in forming relationships _____ (C)

7. When someone is selling to me, I prefer:

To hear their pitch   _____ (A)

To have them ask me questions first _____ (B)

To feel like we are having a
conversation with a purpose   _____ (C)

8. My greatest asset as a sales professional is:

My knowledge _____ (A)

My skills _____ (B)

My personality _____ (C)

9. In terms of my client's goals in life, I believe that these are:

Largely irrelevant to me making
the sale _____ (A)

Somewhat important to know _____ (B)

Crucial to making the sale _____ (C)

10. The most effective strategy for me to improve my sales numbers is to:

Have more appointments _____ (A)

Ask better questions _____ (B)

Know my prospects well _____ (C)

Now add up all of the letters:
Total number for A: _____
Total number for B: _____
Total number for C: _____

A = Traditional sales approach
B = Consultative selling approach
C = Coaching the sale style

This rather transparent assessment should give you some sense of what you believe a true sales professional *should* do. Your honest reflection on how well your behaviors match what you know is right will tell you whether this book will mildly tweak your approach or if there is an opportunity for some major transformation in your approach to selling. If you scored high on the coaching scale, then your philosophy of selling matches perfectly with this book. If you scored high on consultative selling, then your philosophy may need some minor shifting to evolve to the next level. If you scored high on a traditional sales approach, we just encourage you to continue reading to see if you could possibly find benefit from looking at your approach in a different way.

EXERCISE: Coaching Skills Self-Assessment

After your next sales conversation, write down observations concerning your style compared to the coaching skills we discussed in this chapter. Try to make both positive observations and also challenge yourself to some level of growth.

Coaching Skills Observation Form—Self-Assessment

Skill	How did I demonstrate these in my conversation with the prospect (use specific examples)?	How could I have done each of these a little better (give specific suggestions to yourself)?
Understands prospect's goals and motivators		
Asks powerful questions		
Listens well using all three listening styles		
Reflects and clarifies		
Strategizes and problem solves		
Works through blocks to achieving goals		
Moves conversation to action/solution		

| EXERCISE: | Coaching Skills Objective Assessment |

Invite your sales manager, a peer, a friend, or a long-term client with whom you have a completely solid relationship to help you see additional areas for improvement. Either role-play a sales call or have them actually go on a call with you. Immediately afterwards, have them give you feedback using the coaching skills observation form. Ask them to tell you where you did well and where you could have done even better in these areas of coaching skills.

Coaching Skills Observation Form—
to be filled out by observer

Skill	Positive observations of the sales professional doing this well	Suggestions of how the sales professional could have done these even better
Understands prospect's goals and motivators		
Asks powerful questions		
Listens well using all three listening styles		
Reflects and clarifies		
Strategizes and problem solves		
Works through blocks to achieving goals		
Moves conversation to action/solution		

Section II

A Coaching Model
for Sales

Chapter 3

The Coaching Model Phase 1:

Discover

"Good questions outrank easy answers."
—Paul A. Samuelson

"Don't knock the weather. Nine-tenths of the people couldn't start a conversation if it didn't change once in a while."
—Kin Hubbard

Overview

One of the most common responses a salesperson receives is "I'm just looking." Why? Because many people do not believe that sales professionals are really there to help them make their best buying decisions.

The 3D coaching model will make prospects want to talk to you because you will truly help them discover their needs and wants and match those to a purchase that serves them well. In this chapter, we will focus on the first of the three stages to crossing the critical yard–Discover. By uncovering (discovering) your prospects' needs, motivations, and viewpoints, you will be able to serve them better and make the right sale to match their needs. We will look at how to open up the coaching conversation in a way that paints a picture for the prospect to help both you and her understand the needs and desires that will drive the buying decision. We will cover examples that translate across industries to show examples of exact wording that you can work from to find your own style.

As we work through this stage of the model, we will explore more closely the coaching skills of understanding the prospect's motivations/perspectives, listening well, asking powerful questions, and the ability to reflect back to prospects. In each of the stages, we will also explore a specific coaching tool that can help you master the interaction with your prospect or client. In this chapter, we will also explore T.E.A.M. Dynamics, a system for understanding and adapting to different styles of people.

Tales from the Playing Field

"That sales professional was a genius!" were the first words out of his mouth. The financial advisor who said this had been on the phone with one of the wholesalers at my firm and was obviously impressed. "What did he do that was so good?" I asked the advisor. He then went on and on about the style of the sale professional, the great questions he asked, and so on. Then he said the following:

> But the main thing that really impressed me was the way he opened the call. He said that he was prepared to talk about one of your products, but before he did that, he wanted to truly understand my business and where I am focused. Do you know how few wholesalers ever ask me *anything* about my business?
> Where the heck did he learn that? This guy is good. It is obvious that he has been in the business for a long time because he really knows what he is doing. Don't let him get away.

What this financial advisor didn't know was that the wholesaler who called him up was a rookie salesperson who was brand new to the position. It was his first phone call on his first Monday morning. However, this "kid" had been trained in the use of the techniques that we are presenting in this chapter.

Principles

Before we present the first stage of the coaching the sale model, let's reflect on what makes for a great coach.

A Coach Asks Powerful Questions

Coaches ask powerful questions in order to understand the client's goals and motivators. They work with clients to inspire a shared vision. When you are able to tie your product or service with the prospect's goals and visions, then you will make the sale and greatly benefit other human beings. The right question is several times more powerful that the best statement. Questions allow the prospect or client to self-discover solutions, perspectives, and decisions.

Take the following common coaching questions:

What do you want?
What will achieving what you want do for you?
Where, when, and with whom do you want it?
What stops you from having it already?
How are you going to get it?

If asked correctly, these questions are incredibly powerful in a coaching relationship (sales or not). Of course, these questions are not linear and are not to be done in an interrogation-type style, but rather are guideline questions that coaches have in their back pocket when needed to connect to, understand, and motivate a client.

An additional consideration to have when you ask questions of prospects or clients is to know what kind of question that you are asking. Here are five different levels of questions that you could ask a prospect:

Factual—What are you looking to purchase?
Emotional—How do you feel about your shopping experience so far?
Behavioral—What products or services have you looked at so far?

Relational—What role did others play in your purchasing decision?

Spiritual—What need does this potential purchase fulfill for you?

How does it match who you are and want to be?

Coaches know that the right question that leads to self-discovery can change someone's life. Sales professionals who believe in coaching their prospects and clients know that the right question can lead people to the best buying decision for them. When you aid individuals in finding out the best path for themselves, you create loyal and enthusiastic advocates! Powerful questions are the foundation of the discover phase of our model. However, questions without listening skills are useless.

A Coach Listens Well

A coach who is great at asking questions and poor or average at listening is a disaster waiting to happen. Questioning and listening go hand in hand. However, you cannot listen effectively without an open mind. Many people listen mainly for the pause that gives them an opening to talk. Instead of truly listening to the prospect, they are waiting to pounce on the pause in the conversation.

We are sure that the need to be a great listener is not a new concept to any of our readers. However, did you know that there are several things to listen for? You can listen for information. You can listen for emotion. You can listen for behaviors and actions. The important thing is to listen in the way that your prospect wants to be heard. If you are listening for information and they are trying to convey emotion, then the two of you will not be connecting and relating. There are many things to listen for in this conversation:

✓ Assumptions about the product or solution
✓ Previous strategies for solving his problem
✓ Emotions
✓ Blocked thinking
✓ Patterns in handling challenges
✓ Feelings of helplessness and hope
 (so much about sales is building realistic hope)
✓ Competing goals
✓ Possible solutions
✓ Impact of relationships on the sale
✓ Strengths that might aid them in making a great decision
✓ Reactions to you (and then shift your style if they are not connecting with you)
✓ Tentative language ("try to," "maybe," "sort of," etc.)

Also, part of listening is listening to nonverbal behavior. It is crucial to observe these elements as well in order to get clues to what is impacting the person and what might be creating resistance or widening that critical yard.

So how do you listen effectively? What types of things can you observe in a client or prospect? There are several things to be observant about in a client:

✓ Voice
✓ Body language
✓ Involvement with the conversation
✓ Emotions
✓ Confusion or hesitancy
✓ Distraction

Skilled coaches "dance" with their prospects and clients, allowing the client to lead, but continuing to bring the client back to the matter at hand. You will not be able to do this unless you observe and adapt to your prospect's behaviors and attitudes.

Many times just stating the thing that you observed can be helpful. For example, we know of one sales professional who was working with a couple on a sale. He had completed the sale except for the signing of the contract. At that moment, he received a call, which required him to step out of the office for a minute. As he stepped out, he said, "I'm sorry, guys, I will be right back." When he returned to his office, he observed that the couple was not as outgoing as they were initially and their body language seemed cold and distant. Being a skilled coach, he simply asked, "Is everything okay? I'm sensing that something is a little off." At that question, the husband looked at him and said, "My wife is not a guy and she does not appreciate being called one." Of course, the sales professional quickly apologized and took accountability for his shorthand in communication. With that, he was able to quickly rebuild the rapport and made the sale. If he had not observed and commented on the body language and "feel" of the room, he may have easily lost that sale.

In addition to the power of observation, another ability that helps you and your prospect stay connected is our next skill of reflection and clarification.

A Coach Reflects and Clarifies

One of the most simple yet powerful skills in the coach's tool chest is the power of reflecting and summarizing. Surprisingly, we have shadow coached decent sales professionals who for some reason skip this step in the sales conversation. When we talk to them about this, they defend themselves saying, "I know that I heard what the person said, so I didn't need to reflect it back." Our retort is, "How in the world do you expect the client to know that for sure?"

Reflecting back the content of what the prospect or client said gives the person a sense of peace and understanding. Reflecting tells them that you have heard them and understand their needs and challenges. Psychologically, most of us like to hear our own words reflected back to us. But when you watch most team meetings, interactions with couples, and even sales conversations, this skill is not practiced nearly as often as it could and probably should be.

There are two main things that a coach should reflect back:

- Content of what the person said
- Feelings expressed by the person talking about the content

For example, "John, if I understand you correctly, you are saying that your frustration with your old computer has been building for months and just in the last couple of weeks, you have been even more upset about the problems occurring with increased error messages and decreased speed."

And then you would just watch for John's response. This summary and reflection of what John said will have several benefits:

- John feels understood and therefore more at ease
- John is going to nod his head or say yes–that starts a feeling of cooperation and partnership

- John starts trusting you more
- John knows that you were really paying attention to what he said, rather than just waiting to talk
- Many times John will start sharing even more (not even needing you to ask another question to open him up)
- If you have misunderstood John, it gives him to opportunity to correct your impressions and assumptions that will save you from going down the wrong path

There is simply no reason to skip this step in the coaching conversation. If you master the combination of asking powerful questions, listening well, and reflecting/clarifying, then you will be far ahead of most individuals who attempt to make their living in sales. Reflecting and clarifying well is proof that you have asked powerful questions and have listened to the true needs of your client.

The First Stage of the Model
As a reminder, let us mention again what this book is and is not. We are presenting a model and strategy for the interaction with a client or prospect that has shown interest in your product or services. In other words, we are starting with the frame that you both understand why you are meeting. Within that frame, we will provide a step-by-step model for you to consider and adapt to your particular situation. One word of warning: of the three phases in the coaching dialogue, the first stage of Discover is the most complex. There are several different moving parts to the discover phase and at a glance, some can seem elementary or lacking substance. On deeper investigation, some elements can appear to be too complex with too many steps to remember. From training thousands of sales-

people, we can assure you that these steps work and can become second nature and automatic behavior with a little dedication and practice.

Opening the Conversation

The Discover process begins at the start of the sales conversation. This conversation usually begins with some level of small talk. While some people feel uncomfortable with small talk, it is often a necessary part of the selling process. Small talk puts many clients at ease and shows them that you care about more than just making the sale. From the perspective of the sales professional, the goal of small talk is to make an emotional connection with the individual to increase collaboration in the sales process.

One way that we have learned to overcome our dread of small talk is to focus on curiosity. When we go to parties, instead of thinking about what we are going to say to someone, we focus on what we are curious about when we meet someone. Moving our thought process to curiosity takes the pressure off of these social situations and actually makes the experience enjoyable. This is a highly effective way of shifting how you think about small talk. It allows you to enter these situations in a low pressure and intriguing way and ends up showing more respect and interest in the people with whom you are dealing.

Now let's apply curiosity to a sales situation. Before jumping right to business, it would be nice to ask questions about the individual in order to look for commonalities. Sample ways to open up the curious conversation include the following:
- Where are you from?
- What do you do for a living?

- How long have you lived in _____?
- How was your flight coming in?
- How's life been treating you?

More unusual ways to open up the curious conversation are:
- So what is the most intriguing place you been to this year?
- What is the most satisfying part of your job?
- If you could live anywhere in the world and all the logistics would work out, where would you live?
- What is the most unusual thing you have seen in your recent travels?
- What is one thing you have been wanting to create in your life, but you just haven't gotten to yet?

Whether you like these particular questions is irrelevant. You have to find questions that fit *your* style, not ours. However, we hope these will show you the difference between asking a mundane question that just gives you mundane information and asking curiosity-based questions that could open up a gold mine. Curiosity questions are more powerful and more bonding to the prospect than memorized questions with no personal connection to the immediate conversation with the other person. In addition, curiosity questions will help you stay truly interested in the prospect and focused on his or her needs and viewpoints.

TBOP

After working through the initial stages in a conversation using curiosity, the sales professional needs a process to start moving the interaction from chit-chat to the goal of the conversation—pursuing the co-creation of the sale. We refer to our process of doing this with the acronym of TBOP, which stands for

- **T**ransitional opener
- **B**enefits
- **O**bstacles
- **P**lans

The TBOP process is used to fully understand the client or prospect's needs and perspectives in order to best serve him in the sale. It provides a discipline to the sales professional for putting the conversation into a consultative mode. Let's look at each part of the process in detail.

TBOP: Transitional Opener

The "T" of TBOP stands for the *transitional opener*. This is a way to open up the conversation with the sales prospect in a way that will maximize good communication and a firm relationship. If one of my children was going into the sales profession and I could only teach him one skill, that skill would be the transitional opener. It is a powerful technique that completely transforms the conversation with the prospect. The transitional opener does the following:

✓ Smoothly moves you from small talk to business talk
✓ Helps you discipline yourself from falling into the trap of immediately talking too much at the beginning of a sales call
✓ Gets the prospect/client talking first, which reveals to you their current focus and gaps you could help fill

✓ Saves you the embarrassment of completely missing the prospect's goal for the discussion

✓ Helps you figure out what is important to the client and what the client's issues are

✓ Only takes about five seconds to shift the agenda across that critical yard into the prospect's hands

✓ Ensures that if you make a recommendation that it will be the right one

✓ Turns the sales event into a coaching dialogue

The transitional opener follows a "reveal and then reflect" model, in which you are attempting to reveal the prospect's goals and reflect back your understanding of the goals so that the prospect *knows* that you understand the goals and feels positive about the beginning of your interaction.

There are three parts to the transitional opener: 1) statement of confidence; 2) benefit to the client; 3) discovering priorities. The powerful question beneath the transitional opener is "What do you want?"

A Statement of Confidence

A statement of confidence basically tells your prospect that you are ready to inform them and help them in whatever way serves them best and helps set their expectations for the conversation. Many people in a sales situation are expecting the sales professional to dive into his or her explanations of their service or product. Prospects have been conditioned to expect this type of one-way dialogue. In fact, many times in a sales situation, the first thing out of our prospect's mouth is, "So, what's your spiel?" Therefore, if you immediately start the coaching the sale process without a statement of confidence, they may make the false assumption that you aren't prepared, don't have anything to offer them, or are just buying time and distracting the process. So we suggest starting your transitional opener with a statement of confidence, willingness, and preparedness. This helps put your prospect at ease and sets the playing field so that both people understand the process.

Benefit to the Client
In order to avoid resistance or confusion from your prospect, it is important to take a few seconds to explain how you will be better able to serve them if you have more information. You are basically telling your prospects why you are asking them questions rather than talking about your product. This communicates to your prospect the benefits of the coaching the sale approach. Of course, if your prospect resists, then he or she is likely either not interested in your product or service or is looking for more of a traditional sales approach and you should simply switch to a traditional style or move on. However, in our experience, most prospects find this process enlightening, especially if they are familiar with more of a consultative sales model (obviously, since coaching is the next evolution to consultative selling, it does have quite a few things in common with the model). Once you get the prospect's agreement, it is time to move on to discovering priorities.

Discover Priorities and End with a Verbalized Agreement of Goals

This is a very simplistic step that many sales professionals fail to cover at the beginning of their conversation. Amazingly, we have heard many stories of a sales professional going down a path of explaining a certain product or service for minutes before discovering that the client or prospect had a very different goal in mind for their meeting. There are several ways to check in with the prospect's goals. Below are a few examples combining the statement of confidence and the benefit of the coaching the sale style, and discovering priorities by asking about goals. They each follow the basic formula:

- Make a statement of confidence/preparedness
- Say something like, "Before we get started, [name how you are benefiting the prospect by using a questioning approach]"
- Ask a question to uncover the prospect's goals and needs

Examples:

- "I'm prepared to talk with you about _____, and I am confident that our product is the absolute best on the market, but first I want to make sure we are on the same page and make sure it is really the best for your particular needs. So I wanted to ask you, what are you looking for with _____?"
- "I'd be glad to share my ideas with you about _____. But I want to fully understand what you are looking for. Could you tell me what you would like to accomplish with your purchase of _____?"

- "I could certainly share all of the reasons why people buy
  _____, but in order to best assist you, it really helps me to
  understand what you are truly looking for. So tell me, what is
  motivating you to look at a ____?"
- "Just so you know, I am completely prepared to discuss my
  product in detail and share how some other people have
  benefited from it. However, before I begin, I want to make
  sure that I really understand your situation and what you are
  looking for. Therefore, would you mind if I start off asking
  you a few questions? For example, what goal did you have
  in mind when you started shopping around for
  _____?"

In this brief process you are really just looking for the main reason the person is pursuing a purchase. Listen for the most meaningful and personal goal for making this particular purchase. What will your product do for them? How will they use it? In short, why do they want it?

As a test of your listening skills, and even more important, as a technique for connecting with your prospect, it is important to end the transitional opener with a verbalized agreement of the goals that the prospect has stated. Impatient sales professionals will skip this part of the conversation at the cost of connecting with their prospect. You cannot do this. Here is how to successfully verbalize the agreement:

- "So if I understand correctly, the main reason that we are
  meeting today is that your lease is about to expire and you
  are thinking of looking at a new model that will bring you as
  much joy as your last lease."

- "Let me check if I understand your main goal here. It seems like you want to find a financial advisor that is proactive in his approach to your investments because the last advisor you had seemed very passive. It sounds like you feel that his passivity cost you in the performance of your portfolio and you want to make sure that doesn't happen again. You would like to get to know me and understand my philosophy and approach to guiding my clients' investments."
- "So the purpose of our meeting today is to really explore how this business opportunity stacks up against other opportunities you are pursuing. Is that correct?"

Basically all of these can be boiled down to a statement like:
- "If I understand you correctly, you are wanting _____. Is that correct?"

Whether you are just meeting a new prospect or talking to a client for the fifteenth time, the transitional opener is always appropriate and will save you from:
- wasting time
- losing credibility (imagine making a recommendation to a prospect that they already tried that didn't work or fit for them)
- falling into the trap of having to prove yourself to your prospect

Those are the benefits for you, but the client will also benefit because you took the time to really understand what he wants before wasting his time with an irrelevant product pitch.

TBOP: Benefits

Once you form agreement on the goals and the process, then you move to the "B" in the TBOP process—revealing and reflecting the *benefits* for the prospect of reaching his

---

Handling pressure to give your pitch

At times, you will be down to the critical yard and will have resistant prospects that will push you to just give "your pitch." In fact, we are used to working with sales professionals who often only get three to four minutes of an individual's time to make a presentation. They hear, "Just tell me what you've got" frequently while the prospect continues to read his or her email. It is a challenging selling environment. Again, this is common because many sales professionals do just walk in and give their pitch. Sales professionals have inadvertently trained many clients to expect a pitch. When you are greeted with this type of resistance *before* you have tried a transitional opener, then simply say something along the lines of:

"I am certainly prepared to talk with you about our services today, but I think it is presumptuous of me to assume that my product is right for you until I understand more about what you are looking for. I find that my clients benefit more from me having a good understanding of their unique situation and challenges than just assuming I know what is best for them. The process I use will help both of us realize if there is a good match. If it is okay with you, I would like to ask you a few more questions. How would you feel about that?"

However, if once you have made a transitional opener the prospect continues to ask for your pitch, then we encourage you to simply shift your style to what she is looking for. It would not serve you well to fight her on this point. All other issues aside, we trust that you know your industry and your prospects. You have some that will only want a presentation and others that will welcome our coaching approach. It is more difficult with those individuals who do not know you and have not been introduced to you by a trusted third party. Simply trust your judgment and choose the right approach for the right prospect. However, learn this model so that you have the discipline to take a coaching approach as your automatic stance with a prospect unless directed otherwise. Also, remember that our model is not built to be a prospecting tool focusing on cold calls, but is rather for sales professionals who really want to impact clients and develop long-term relationships.

goals (in relation to the product or service you are representing). In this part of the conversation, you encourage the client to paint a picture or form a vision of the benefits of reaching his goal. You do this to help the client fully "feel" why he wants to make some sort of purchase. This increases the prospect's motivation and also continues to increase your bonding process with him. Examples of questions that will help reveal the benefits are below:

- If you could have the type of relationship that you are looking for with a _____, how will that serve your plans for your life?
- What are the benefits for you of buying a _____?
- What is your vision for having a _____?
- Why are you looking to buy a _____?

Let's make sure you have mastered these general questions. Take a look at the sidebar titled "Industry-Specific Questions" to get a sense of how to apply these questions to specific industries.

When you ask these questions, you are looking for deep emotional answers instead of just surface issues. For example, if you ask, "What will buying a new Lexus do for you?" you would much rather get an answer like "It will help me balance my care for my family and my own desires by

Industry-Specific Questions

Financial services
- What will it do for you to have all your assets with one advisor?
- If you could have the type of relationship that you are looking for with an advisor, how will that serve your plans for your life?

Coaching and training
- What is your vision for having a coach help you focus on your goals?
- What are the benefits for you of training your sales reps on confidence skills?

Network marketing
- What will it do for you to have your own business?
- What is your vision for having a flexible schedule that you control?

Automobile industry
- Why are you looking to buy a Lexus?
- What will having a convertible do for you?

Insurance
- What will it do for you to have a policy that covers your family's housing and future college needs?
- What are the main reasons that you want to buy a policy?

Real Estate
- What will having the added space do for you?
- How does buying a larger house fit into your plans for the future?

Obviously we could go on, but we hope we have demonstrated for you that these questions (like all of this book) translate well across any industry that involves sales.

combining performance and safety" than "I will get a great car." The deeper the answer, the more helpful you can be to truly meet your prospect's needs, which creates a client for life. Now, not all prospects will offer up a deep answer at first (especially if you have not built enough trust). Therefore, keep asking the questions until you see that "glimmer in the eyes" that says you have found the real benefit for which they are looking.

Following the same reveal and reflect model as the transitional opener, reveal or discover the information and then paraphrase it back to the prospect. Do not move on to the next part of TBOP until you reflect back and summarize what you heard your prospect say and get verbal agreements or head nods that indicate that you are both on the same page.

On a side note, later in this process, we will show you how to build powerful stories about the benefits of your products or services using something we call the three-point play. Once you have done that, you can return to this section and think about discovery questions that are specific to the benefits of your product/service.

TB**O**P: Obstacles

Once you have agreement, you then move on to the "O" of the TBOP process—revealing and reflecting the prospect's *obstacles* to achieving their goals. Obviously, something has either prevented them from making this purchase in the past or has potential for blocking them from making the purchase in the present. The obstacles could be anything from financial concerns to differences in buying preferences in families to someone's own guilt about treating themselves.

Why is it important to understand the client's previous obstacles before pursuing the co-creation of the sale? Basically, you want to understand what has stopped them from making the purchase (and thus reaching their goals) in the past and reveal any current obstacles that could prevent them from purchasing now. If these are not revealed, then you have potential land mines that will decrease your ability to effectively match your product and services to their needs.

Questions you might ask are as simple as:

• What has kept you from getting _____ before?

• What would prevent you from _____ now?

Some industry examples of obstacle-revealing questions:

Information Technology
- What has kept you from getting your own server before?
- What would prevent you from upgrading your system now?

Mortgage business
- What has kept you from getting a loan before?
- What would prevent you from buying a new house now?

So let's say that what has kept your client from buying life insurance in the past is that his spouse doesn't like to discuss the possibility of one of them dying and therefore thinks that talking about insurance is unnecessary and uncomfortable. That information is crucial. The simple question of "What has kept you from making this purchase in the past?" could reveal this to you. Without it, you may never invite the spouse in for a meeting and may miss the chance to serve these clients. Knowing the obstacles allows you to brainstorm approaches and solutions with your prospects to overcome them. Not knowing the obstacles means you are standing in a minefield and depending on luck to be successful.

Again using the reveal/reflect method of the TBOP model, you must stop to summarize and paraphrase the prospect's statements concerning obstacles before moving on to the "P" segment of the TBOP formula: plan. In our previous example, you might say something like, "So if I understand you correctly, you have not bought insurance in the past because you spouse dislikes talking about the topic and you have not felt comfortable making a decision until she is on board with this. Is that correct?" Once the prospect indicates that you understand the block, then you and he could work on potential strategies to overcome the obstacle.

TBO**P**: Plans

The fourth part of the TBOP process is to ask questions about the prospect's *plans.* Using the reveal and reflect model, you want to reveal any of the prospect's previous attempts to purchase and reveal any current plans for purchasing. Example coaching questions would be:

- What have you done so far in your search for _____?
- What is your plan currently in terms of getting _____?

By knowing your prospect's previous and current plans, you can find out if there is a need to frame your product or services against a competitor's, discover how serious your prospect is about making a purchasing decision, and discover additional information that may help you work more

Some industry examples of determining plans:

Banking
- What have you done so far in your search for a relationship with a bank?
- What is your plan currently in terms of getting your different needs for financial services met?

Coaching and training
- What have you done so far in your search for a coach?
- What is your plan currently in terms of getting conflict management training for your team?

effectively with your prospect. Without this information, you may lose the sale due not to skill, but to a crucial piece of missing information.

Another benefit of addressing previous plans with a prospect is that you ensure that you are not walking them down a road they have been on before. It is quite embarrassing to go on for ten minutes about a potential solution with a prospect only to discover that they have heard that solution before and have rejected it. Knowing the past and current plans allows for a more efficient conversation and one truly tailored to the prospect's needs.

As with other steps in the TBOP process and the rest of this book, these coaching questions cross industries and situations extremely well and will reveal useful information for the sales professional to address with his or her prospect. The TBOP process is the setup for your presentation. It creates the foundation of the sales call and allows you to proceed with effective and relevant dialogue with the client.

TBOP Summarized

So to summarize the TBOP process:

The goal of TBOP is to fully understand client needs and perspectives.

The process consists of revealing, listening, and reflecting back the prospect's perspectives using four steps:

Transitional Opener—Start with a statement of confidence, willingness, and preparedness; move to asking about goals; and end with verbalized agreement of goals.

Benefits—Reveal and reflect the benefits of the client's purchasing goal to help the client paint a clear and compelling vision of the benefits of reaching his or her goal.

Obstacles—Reveal and reflect obstacles to making the purchase.

Plans—Reveal and reflect any previous attempts to purchase and any current plans for purchasing.

After completing the TBOP process, you then move to the Discuss phase of the coaching conversation and then eventually to the Decide phase. The figure below, which was developed for financial advisors, summarizes the process given your prospect's openness to a coaching process.

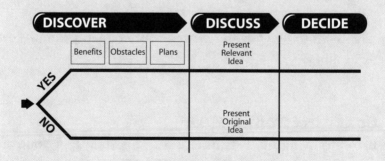

So how important is the TBOP process? A simple and true story demonstrates the dangers of not following this process. Mark was a friend of mine who I had known for almost fifteen years. One day, we were just hanging out and I happened to ask him what he was working on with his clients. He mentioned that he was working on a huge 401(k) rollover worth $150 million. He shared with me the product that he was planning to use for this project, which happened to come from one of my company's main competitors. Fortunately, I had just come out of a meeting where I learned that our company's product was greatly outperforming the one from our competitor. I simply mentioned this to Mark and asked him if he would consider our product. There was absolutely no sales pitch; we simply discussed the project and the products in a conversational way.

That conversation resulted in a $25 million order for my company. All I did was ask Mark what he was doing (sort of an informal TBOP). Amazingly, the salesperson who was assigned to Mark's account never asked Mark about his business priorities. It is not Mark's responsibility to tell our salesperson what he is working on. As sales professionals, we must ask the right questions. Had our sales professional followed the TBOP process, he would have impacted the sale. By not following the process, our company almost lost $25 million.

Coaching Tool: TEAM

Before moving on, let's discuss an important tool you can use. For each of the phases in the 3D coaching the sale model, we will be sharing a coaching tool that we think is invaluable to the process. For the Discover phase of the model, we believe that one of the most important tools in the coaching arsenal is TEAM.

When you have a product or service, the features are standardized, but the benefits must be customized to the prospect. Imagine that you are selling a car to an individual. How do you know what features to highlight? Certainly, you will have solid information from your discovery questions, but how else could you determine what to highlight? For example, some people would want to hear more about the safety of the vehicle for their family, some about the efficiency, some about the research, and others about the cutting-edge technology of the car. The individual's behavioral style will tell you a lot about how to focus your discussion. TEAM is a process of determining your behavioral style and the preferred style of your prospect. It is based on the theory that people are more comfortable around people like them. The more you can speak the behavioral language of your prospect, the more your prospect will trust you and want to work with you. It is like going to a foreign country. If you knew how to speak the language, why wouldn't you? It is just common sense.

However, you don't need to be from different countries to speak different languages. Sometimes our behavioral style will dictate our way of communicating. For example, take two simple continuums: speed and focus. Some people are very fast and impulsive. They tend to be dominant, impatient, and talk quickly. On the other end of the continuum are people who are much more hesitant and methodical. They tend to be more passive, reserved, and speak carefully. Neither is better or worse; they are just different in their presentation of speed. On the other continuum, you have a difference in focus. Some people tend to be very logic and task-focused (i.e., what needs to be done) while others tend to be people/relationship focused (i.e., how the people fit into it). Again, neither is better; we need both types of focus in the world. Interestingly, if you put these two continuums together, you will come up with four main styles that people tend to show. These are shown on the chart below.

	Methodical-Hesitant	Impulsive-Dominant
People/Relationship Focus	Togetherness Person	Motivator
Logic/Task Focus	Analyzer	Enterpriser

Let's take a look at each of the styles in more detail.

Togetherness Person— Methodical Pace/People Focus

People showing togetherness styles want to achieve stability in relationships and in life. They work to accomplish this by cooperating with others. They tend to be even keeled, non-threatening, and calm. In conversation, they are respectful, responsive, and great listeners. You will notice that they are team players and look out for the needs of others. They tend to dislike change and conflict and do not like pushy sales professionals. Unfortunately, they are not always assertive in their needs, so they may disappear as a prospect and never tell you why. If you are selling a minivan to a togetherness person, you might emphasize the safe trips and relationship memories he would experience with his family. If you are in network marketing, you might focus on operating a business from your home to provide flexibility for family interaction and time.

Enterpriser—Fast Pace/Task Focus
People showing enterpriser styles want to get results by overcoming challenges in life. They work to accomplish this by taking action and going for immediate results. They tend to be candid, direct, and highly confident. In conversation they are confrontational, abrupt, and often interrupt. You will notice that they are decisive and like to take risks. They tend to dislike weakness and people trying to control them and do not respect sales professionals who lack confidence. If they feel like you are trying to take advantage of them in a sales situation, they will come out of the corner fighting. If you are selling a minivan to an enterpriser, you might emphasize the fact that you can get everyone in the car so that no one needs to caravan and you can get to your destination more quickly. In network marketing, it would be wise to focus on the ability to own your own business and control your success.

Analyzer—Methodical Pace/Task Focus
People showing analyzer styles want to achieve high standards and accuracy. They work to accomplish this by

working within the rules and doing things the "right" way. They tend to be reserved, meticulous, and somewhat rigid. In conversation, they are deliberate, hesitant, and focused. You will notice that they are cautious, precise, and diplomatic. They tend to dislike ambiguity and uncertainty and do not like sales professionals who do not have the expertise that they are looking for. Unfortunately, they can be black-and-white in their thinking at times and can be difficult to bond with quickly. If you are selling a minivan to an analyzer, you might emphasize how your model saves on gas and no one would be late to a gathering because everyone would be in the same car. A network marketer might focus on the systems and processes developed by the home company, creating a predictable path to success.

Motivator—Fast Pace/People Focus

People showing motivator styles want to achieve recognition and success by impacting and motivating others. They work to accomplish this by being energetic and persuasive. They tend to be enthusiastic, animated, and playful. In conversation, they are flexible, expressive, and unfocused. You will notice that they are charming and free-spirited. They tend to fear rejection and negativity and do not like sales professionals who are boring in their presentation. Unfortunately, you may have the best product in the world, but if your energy is "wrong" in presenting it, you will lose the sale. If you are selling a minivan to a motivator, then you might emphasize how the optional DVD addition creates a party in a car and paint a picture of road trips with popcorn, pop, and a good movie. In network marketing, the motivator would be most interested in the public recognition given at the annual conference and perhaps the fun trips for top performers.

Again, there is no right or wrong style. Each has strengths and each has weaknesses. Truthfully, many of us are combinations of these different styles. The important thing is not which style you tend to prefer, but rather your ability to adapt to the style of your prospect. Just imagine a high Motivator presenting to a high Analyzer. The Motivator may be showing enthusiasm, friendliness, and energy, which may draw another Motivator closer, but what impact do you think it has on the Analyzer? It pushes him away! The same is true for an Enterpriser who comes on too strongly with a Togetherness Person: the person will not feel comfortable and will just shut down.

The most effective coaches realize that they have pieces of each style inside and learn how to pull out the style of the prospect with whom they are dealing. Now, we could write a whole book and do whole-day programs on styles, so we will not be able to cover everything here, but below are a few tips to keep in mind.

Looking at Your Own Style

You may experience the following challenges as a sales professional given your style profile:
- T: You may come across as too indirect or wishy-washy.
- E: You may seem pressuring, insensitive, and impatient with customers.
- A: You might come across as cold or too detailed.
- M: You can seem not detailed enough in your presentation or too energetic/flaky.

These would be important perceptions to be aware of. Is this how you want your prospect to perceive you? If not, then you need to focus on their style instead of your own. You can get an informal sense of a client's style by simply going back to our two continuums:

- Is the person fast/impulsive or hesitant/methodical?
- Is the person more focused on the task/logic or on people?

If you can answer these two questions, then you can get a sense of their style. Also, the prospect's style will be revealed to you if you do the TBOP effectively. The way that they answer your questions and the things they emphasize will reveal all you need to know.

Tips for dealing with the different styles
Here are a few quick tips for dealing with the different styles.

Togetherness Prospect

Do:

- show caring
- cover the process in a step-by-step manner
- introduce new ideas slowly
- listen to their concerns
- be sensitive to their feelings

Do not:

- push them into deciding
- speak too quickly
- focus on the task at the sake of personally connecting
- show disregard for others

Enterpriser Prospect

Do:

- show respect
- be concise
- introduce new ideas with confidence
- focus on results
- let them lead as much as possible

Do not:

- corner them
- appear weak
- be lured into an argument or competition
- take too much of their time or focus on feelings

Analyzer Prospect

Do:

- focus on the details
- cover the process methodically and analytically
- introduce new ideas by comparing them with proven methods
- know your facts
- be respectful of their expertise

Do not:

- try to sell with your personality
- be scattered in your presentation
- push for a decision
- use poorly organized materials

Motivator Prospect

Do:

- show enthusiasm
- cover the process energetically and quickly
- be positive and fun

- be flexible
- help them visualize the future

Do not:
- overload them with details
- be boring
- be too task-oriented
- show any signs of rejection

These are general principles to be aware of when inter-acting with different behavioral styles. Interacting with your clients without understanding their style is like trying to chop wood with a dull axe. However, if you adapt to the style by shifting tone, pace, and emphasis, then you are sharpening your axe and cutting wood with less effort and greater efficiency. If you have addressed the style of the client and have followed the TBOP process, then you are ready to move on to the next phase of the 3D model.

Segueing to the Next Phase of the 3D Model: Discuss

Cars require oil to run effectively and efficiently. The sound of gears grinding can send chills up your spine. What oil is for the gears in your car, the segue is for the conversation. The lack of a segue or a poor segue can bring an otherwise smooth conversation to a grinding halt. A nice segue makes the conversation flow freely and without awkwardness.

For coaching that sale, the segue that we will use between the Ds of the 3D model is the reflective review.

The purpose of the reflective review is to make sure that you fully understand the client's perspectives and motives and are able to form a collaborative spirit to the discussion before advancing the conversation. An example would be:

> If I understand you correctly, you are saying that you want _____ (name goal) because it will give you _____ (name benefits) and that you have been stopped in the past because _____ (name obstacles) when you have done _____ (name plans). Is that right (get agreement)? Okay, well what I would like to do then is for us to take your thoughts and some of my ideas and see if we can collaborate on a good solution for you. How open do you feel to looking at that right now?

If the prospect is resistant to moving to the discuss phase of the 3D model, then you need to go back to the beginning. For example, you might say, "Obviously I have missed something in our previous discussion, so help me understand, what are you really looking for right now?" You then walk through the TBOP process again to uncover what you overlooked in the conversation or to determine if the prospect is not really in the position to discuss buying the product or service at the current time.

Another optional technique is to add a story of aiding a past client with these goals to show that you have been able to help others with these goals and this buying decision. Some have used this technique in the past as a manipulative strategy. We are not advocating that at all! Rather, we are suggesting the use of this technique called the "bandwagon effect" merely to help the prospect or client feel more comfortable. Truthfully, most of us tend to buy what others are buying. We want to know that we are making wise decisions, and if no one else is buying your product, then we would doubt the wisdom of making this purchase. We want reassurance. We feel better knowing that four out of five dentists recommend a certain type of gum or that 25 percent of new cars sold are a certain brand. The bandwagon effect lets us know that it is okay to make the purchase. So do not hesitate to drop names and numbers that would increase the individual's feeling of security.

As we end this chapter, we have some exercises for you to complete around the TBOP process. We also have included an assessment of your style. Use this to determine your own TEAM style and how you might adapt to become even more effective as a sales professional.

EXERCISE: Creating Your Own Industry-Specific TBOP

Throughout this chapter, we have offered general questions along with versions specific to several industries. One of the most effective ways to master the TBOP process is to go through and create questions that you can specifically use in your position and industry. So walk through the TBOP stages below and create questions for your future use. If you feel stumped on any of these, simply go back to the examples found earlier in the chapter.

Transitional Opener—Create a statement of confidence, willingness, and preparedness, name the benefit of your approach, and ask a question that helps discover the prospect's priorities. End with a statement of agreement on those goals (you will have to remember a recent sales discussion to create that agreement):

_____

_____

_____

_____

_____

_____

_____

_____

_____

_____

_____

_____

_____

Benefits—Take the following questions and adapt them to become common questions that you could have at your disposal for your product or service.

The general question	Your adapted version for your industry
What will it do for you to have a _____?	
If you could have the type of relationship that you are looking for with a _____, how will that serve your plans for your life?	
What are the benefits for you of buying a _____?	
What is your vision for having a _____?	
Why are you looking to buy a _____?	
How does buying _____ fit into your plans for the future?	
What are the main reasons that you want to buy _____?	

Obstacles—Take the two general questions we have below and expand on them or improve them for your product or service:

Our version:
What has kept you from getting _____ before?

Your version:

_____ ?

Our version:
What would prevent you from _____ now?

Your version:

_____ ?

Plans—Do the same for the plans part of the TBOP process (remember that although this may seem simple, the idea is to introduce repetition of the concept to help master it).

Our version:
What have you done so far in your search
for _____?

Your version:

_____ ?

Our version:
What is your plan currently in terms of
getting _____?

Your version:

_____ ?

EXERCISE: Creating Your Segue to the Next Phase of the 3D Model

In order to smoothly transition to the discussion phase of the 3D model, work up a sample segue. For this exercise, you will need to think of a recent sales situation in order to fill in the example more completely. Remember that the segue is the oil that makes transitioning in the conversation go well. So recall a recent sales conversation and fill in the following formula:

If I understand you correctly, you are saying that you want...

_____

_____

_____

(Name goal)

...because it will give you...

_____

_____

_____

(Name benefits)

...and that you have been stopped in the past because...

_____

_____

_____

(Name obstacles)

...when you have done...

_____

_____

_____

(Name plans)

Is that right (get agreement)? Okay, well what I would like to do then is for us to...

_____

_____

_____

(Name intent such as "see if we can collaborate on a good solution for you")

How...

_____

_____

_____

(Ask prospect's permission to proceed with the discussion)

EXERCISE: Your TEAM Style

Take the following assessment to get a sense of your TEAM style.

Directions: Read each group of four phrases lettered A through D. Mark a "4" next to the phrase that describes you best, a "3" next to the phrase that describes you second best etc... You should have just one "4", one "3", one "2" and one "1" marked in each group. Once you've completed all the groups, add your total score for A's, B's, C's, and D's, and record it at the bottom of the sheet. Your total scores for all four letters should add up to 120.

LEAST = 1   2   3   4   MOST

A ____ True to Friends   A ____ Understanding

B ____ Innovator   B ____ Takes Charge

C ____ Thinks Things Through   C ____ Accurate

D ____ Energetic   D ____ Achiever

A ____ Thoughtful of Others   A ____ Giving

B ____ Daring   B ____ Does Own Thing

C ____ Wants All Information   C ____ Deliberate

D ____ Laughs Easily/Witty   D ____ Articulate

A ____ Will Do as Instructed

B ____ Risk Taker

C ____ Wants Things Exact

D ____ Persuasive

A ____ Interested in People

B ____ Refuses to Give Up

C ____ Humble

D ____ Leads the Pack

A ____ Listens and Remains Calm

B ____ Wants to Win

C ____ Deliberate and Cautious

D ____ Enthusiastic

A ____ Flows with the Crowd

B ____ Strong Personality

C ____ Dependable

D ____ Interesting Person

A ____ Hides Feelings

B ____ Courageous and Unafraid

C ____ High Standards

D ____ Likes to Talk

A ____ Does Not Rock the Boat

B ____ Speaks Openly and Boldly

C ____ Plays by the Rules

D ____ Gets Others Involved

A ____ Friendly to Others

B ____ Decisive

C ____ Wants Order

D ____ Outgoing

A ____ Wants Others Involved

B ____ Results Driven

C ____ Difficult Time Deciding

D ____ Optimistic

TOTALS: A=____   B=____   C=____   D=____

Directions: Transfer your A, B, C, and D scores from the quiz. Draw a dot on the corresponding graph line. Then connect the dots to create a graph of your personality profile.

48. _____
47. _____
46. _____
45. _____
44. _____
43. _____
42. _____
41. _____
40. _____
39. _____
38. _____
37. _____
36. _____
35. _____
34. _____
33. _____
32. _____
31. _____
30. _____
29. _____
28. _____
27. _____
26. _____
25. _____
24. _____
23. _____
22. _____
21. _____
20. _____
19. _____
18. _____
17. _____
16. _____
15. _____
14. _____
13. _____
12. _____

Togetherness   Enterpriser   Analyzer   Motivator

A Total ____   **B Total** ____   **C Total** ____   **D Total** ____

EXERCISE: Shifting Your Style

How might you want to shift your style given the style of your prospect? Use the following chart to reason through this exercise and come up with methods to help you be effective with all styles.

Prospect's style	What tendency of yours do you need to decrease to best connect to this style?	What behaviors should you increase to relate to this style?	What words might help you connect best with the person?
Togetherness person			
Enterpriser			
Analyzer			
Motivator			

Chapter 4

The Coaching Model Phase 2:

Discuss

"Advice is like snow: the softer it falls, the longer it
dwells upon and the deeper it sinks into the mud."
—Samuel Taylor Coleridge

"No one wants advice, only corroboration."
—*The Winter of Our Discontent*, John Steinbeck

Overview

Once you have discovered the prospect's goals, benefits to
achieving their goals, obstacles to purchasing, and past and
current purchasing plans, it is now time to move into a truly
interactive discussion. It is at this point that even those sales professionals who are decent at a consultative-selling style often
break down and lose the true spirit of the consultative sale. Often
after gathering the initial information, the interaction between
the sales professional and prospect loses any appearance of a discussion and instead becomes a platform for the sales professional

to sell. Even worse, the attempt to sell often boils down into a "shotgun" approach of throwing out many multiples of benefits to the prospect with a hope of matching up to his or her needs. In the Discuss stage of the 3D coaching conversation, we will show you another way to interact with your prospect or client, one that will help you clearly describe the benefits of your product or service to a prospect while the two of you *co-create* the sale. The model for this part of the conversation is *share, pause, and agree* (which we will explain in more detail as we progress). We will also explore how a coach helps a prospect strategize, problem-solve, and work through blocks to their goals. Finally, we will look at how to use storyboarding as a coaching tool to aid you in matching solutions to the prospect's challenges.

Tales from the Playing Field

Why did Hillary Clinton fail in her attempts with the 1993–4 health care reform effort? Well, you will get many different opinions about that, but one possibility has to do with her ability to sell it. The Clinton health care plan can be found in a 1,431-page document and was presented using such phrases as:

- regional alliance health plans
- premium-based financing
- transitional insurance reform
- coordination with COBRA
- continuation coverage

One thousand, four hundred thirty-one pages, using terms that leave most of us spinning from confusion! How could something this confusing have a chance of "selling through" the government? Of course, this is normal behavior for the government, but what does this have to do with sales?

A few months ago, I was approached by a sales professional named Larry. Larry represented a testing company and was pursuing me to become a distributor for their leadership assessment product. I had agreed to meet with Larry and was actually interested in finding a good leadership product. That is, until Larry started talking. In a fifteen-minute monologue, he must have listed twenty random and unrelated benefits of using this product. I only understood parts of a few of the benefits because he kept using unfamiliar terms specific to his test. I wish I could recreate them for you here, but I could not remember these terms if my life depended on it. And as the icing on the cake, he never once asked me why I had shown interest in meeting him in the first place. His perplexing and meandering monologue left me confused. A confused prospect does not trust. An untrusting prospect will not buy. Larry left without a sale. If I read him correctly, he was as confused about his product as I was.

Principles

The question to ask yourself is this: "How well do you clearly, concisely, and in a well connected manner articulate your product or service?" In addition, are you able to do this in dialogue with your prospect, or do you fall into a monologue? In this chapter, we will help you clearly *discuss* your product with your prospect and hone in on three benefits that match his or her needs.

Coaches help clients (and sales professionals help prospects) strategize solutions to their pains and challenges. In the purist form of coaching, the coach is not the main one strategizing, but rather acts as a powerful focusing lens to help the client solve his or her own problem. Ideally, the more a sales professional can apply this to the sales discussion the better. The more the prospect can self-discover the solution to the challenges, the more powerful the sale and buying decision.

However, realistically, companies and individuals often speak to sales professionals because they want their expertise and knowledge. To have the sales conversation and never offer this would be ludicrous. For example, when coaching individuals in companies, we tend to use the purist form of coaching most of the time to help clients self-discover. However, when talking to a company representative about hiring us for coaching, we definitely share our thoughts and expertise on solutions to their challenges. Basically, we follow the coaching the sale model that we will be presenting to you, and find it extremely effective. If we stuck with a pure coaching model, we doubt that many companies would hire us. They want to hear your expertise. The secret is to only share that expertise after adequately gathering, listening, reflecting, and making sure that you are completely on the same page.

What we will be presenting in this chapter has some strong subtleties that may not be apparent at first glance. If at any point you find yourself thinking, "I do that already," we want to encourage you to challenge that thought. Ask yourself a self-coaching question such as, "How might this be different (even slightly) from what I usually do?" You will find a much better payoff utilizing this kind of attitude than discounting the information.

The model for interaction in the Discuss phase of the 3D model is **share/pause/agree**. Obviously in a sales situation, at some point, the sales professional must share some information (this is not the case when doing pure coaching). The difference between our coaching model and the previous consultative selling models is the level of interaction that occurs at the share phase between the sales professional's solutions and the prospect's goals. We call this the three-point play.

The Three-Point Play

The three-point play breaks down your solution into three simple points that can address the client's needs. All coaches and sales professionals know it is crucial to understand the strengths and weaknesses of your product or service. Many also know how important it is to have a story built around these strengths. However, sometimes professionals will ramble on about the five, six, or seven benefits of their product. The human mind gets bored easily and by the time you get to your fourth benefit, all the prospect is hearing is blah, blah, blah.

The human mind can take three things and these three must be compelling. They must be compelling facts about your product or service with benefits connected to each.

The three-point play technique solves the sales profession-al's challenge of having too many things to say about their product and keeps them focused on mentioning the bene-fits. This is why the TBOP of the discover phase of the 3D models has you asking the prospect about the benefits they are looking for; it helps you match well to serve them best and make the sale easy.

At the end of this chapter, we present a technique called storyboarding that you can use to help generate the three things you want to say about your product or service. This coaching tool can also help you discover if you are failing to sell the benefits of your product and service as well as you might be able. Once you do this exercise, you will know your top three benefits. However, for now, let's assume that you know your client's goals or needs and you are ready to offer a possible solution using your products or services. Sales professionals utilizing the consultative selling model are used to the concept of taking the time to match up goals and benefits. However, the coaching model shows strength in *how* you connect these.

Making Smooth Connections

In the last chapter, we used the analogy of oil to represent shifting gears between discovering goals with the clients and moving to discussing solutions. We can use this same analo-gy to represent connecting solutions.

Oil makes machines work more. The smooth connection is crucial to functioning well. It is no different in a sales sit-uation. Imagine the missed opportunities for the sales pro-fessional who:

• offers solutions with no reference to the prospect's goals

- forces solutions to match up with prospect goals artificially
- tries to match solutions to prospect goals, but does so awkwardly or confusingly

It would be like metal rubbing against metal.

So let's focus on this next phase of the coaching conversation. By this time in the meeting, you have done the groundwork. You know most of what you need to know to make a sale that serves you and the prospect. Now it is time to discuss.

It is unfortunate that many sales professionals do not take the time to *master* this phase of the conversation. The discussion phase, when mastered, not only leads to a solid relationship, but can create raving fans for you as the person to go to when someone has a challenge and needs help. As mentioned, the three-point play is the technique that makes this happen.

The Formula for Making the Three-Point Play

What follows is a simplistic formula for connecting well with the prospect's needs.

Share point #1
Connect it back to the initial goals (making sure you have good oil, i.e., the connection is smooth)
Check in with the prospect with a question

Share point #2
Again, connect it back to the initial goals (again making sure the connection is smooth)
Again, check in with the prospect with a new question

Share point #3
Again, connect it back to the initial goals (again making sure the connection is smooth)
Again, check in with the prospect with a new question

Let's walk through an example to help demonstrate this. Here is how someone attempting to recruit someone into a network marketing business might utilize the approach. At this point, the person in the network marketing group has spent the time and discipline in the Discover phase to learn that the prospect has three main goals for her life (while you do not have to connect your benefits back to more than one of your client's goals, we are going to demonstrate connecting back to three goals for the sake of variety):

1. To have financial freedom
2. To have control over her schedule
3. To be in control of the level of her own success

Previous obstacles found in the Discover phase were being stuck in a job for the last ten years with an overbearing and micromanaging boss and hitting the ceiling on her salary. The benefits of achieving her goals include more time with her children, the ability to take trips and vacations when she wants to, and being free of any type of influence that would make her feel like she is working at a lower level than she should. Her previous plans have mainly been dreaming about it and this is the first time she is really branching out to do something about it.

The network marketing sales professional has done his homework and knows the strength of his business (especially if he has used our storyboarding process at the end of this chapter). Below represents his side of the conversation:

Share point #1: One of the greatest advantages of this opportunity is that the top people have built a consistent revenue stream that will go on even after they retire in the business.

Connect it back to the initial goals: I know that you mentioned that financial freedom is very important to you, which is why I thought you might be intrigued by this part of the business.

Check in with the prospect with a question: How does the idea of reoccurring revenue even in retirement fit with what you are looking for with financial freedom?

That was the sharing portion. Now you pause to give the prospect time to think through and answer your question. Make sure that you are in agreement on that solution meeting the goal before moving on to the next point in the three-point play. Ask:

So it sounds like we are in agreement that reoccurring passive revenue would have significant impact on your future financial freedom. Is that right?

If the answer is yes, then move on the point #2.

Share point #2: Another part of the business that I think you will find intriguing is that you get to decide your own office hours. You get to decide when you work and when you play. There is no one standing over your shoulder or watching you punch the clock. It is part of the reason that we really look to attract people with a strong entrepreneurial track to their personalities. People without the entrepreneurial spirit tend to have problems disciplining themselves to hold the schedule they think they should. We are looking for people that want that level of responsibility.

Connect it back to the initial goals: I hope that you can see that I am really trying to address the goals that you shared at the beginning of our conversation. I know you mentioned that you would like to be able to control your own schedule, and with us, it is definitely fully in your hands when you work, when you spend time with family, when you vacation, etc.

Check in with the prospect with a question: What would be your vision for work hours, vacation, etc., if you joined us and had this complete control?

After sharing, pause and come to agreement on how your service meets the goal. Then move on to point three of the three-point play.

Share point #3: Obviously, your schedule is just part of what you would control if you came on with us. One of the things that is most meaningful to me is that no one decides how successful I can become. There is no ceiling on my earnings except for the one that I put there myself by my choices with my focus and time.

Connect it back to the initial goals: I know that you have been frustrated by the limits that others have put on your earnings, and I know that you have a strong desire to grow to the level you want to grow to.

Check in with the prospect with a question: What questions do you have about your ability to decide your own level of success with my company?

Additional questions that you could ask at any of the three points that would encourage a full discussion include:

- What are your feelings so far on this idea?
- How am I doing in addressing your main goals here?
- Before I go into more detail, I would like to hear your reaction to this. What are you thinking about this idea?

By asking these questions, you are constantly checking in with your prospect, which is both respectful and guarantees that you will stay on track with him or her. Of course, the form of your questions is also very important.

Open-Ended Questions

Astute observers will notice that, with the exception of the segue between points #1 and #3, all of the questions are open-ended questions. This is purposeful and very important. Open-ended questions open up and encourage discussion (which is crucial for crossing the critical yard). Yes/no questions are more effective for bringing closure to a point in the discussion and moving on to the next point. Unfortunately, our research shows that it is *very* difficult for many sales professionals to ask open-ended questions. Traditional sales professionals are use to "leading the witness" and trying to control the process with yes/no questions. You can't blame them—they have been trained to do this! In fact, when we do workshops on coaching the sale, we do role-plays to help participants practice the skills. One of the requests we make of coaches is that they take on a "deer in the headlights" look when their partner asks them a yes/no question. Within minutes, we have lots of odd-looking people in the room. However, the exercise is invaluable for helping the coach realize when he or she is asking closed-ended questions. It also demonstrates in a dramatic fashion how these types of questions can take an otherwise fluid conversation to a screeching halt.

Having a True Discussion

Once you master the open-ended questions, then you can strategically use the yes/no questions between points in the three-point play. Once you have done your three points, discussed them fully with the prospect, and made sure that you matched your solutions well to their needs, it is time to move to the deciding stage. Again, you must focus on the segue as the oil to keep the gears lubricated as you are about to make the shift. At this stage, the best segue is the reflective review. The reflective review summary is basically:

It sounds like we are in agreement on (Point #1, Point #2, Point #3) matching up well with (client's goal or goals). Is that correct?

The reflective review is symbolic of the relationship between you and the prospect in this stage of the coaching sales process. You continually make sure that you are still in contact with the client.

I once had a massage therapist as a coaching client. She was trying to build her business and was describing her approach to her work. One thing that she emphasized was that when she was massaging a client, she would keep one hand on them at all times. She emphasized the importance of continually letting her clients know she was there and was connected with them.

Now, we are not suggesting that you hold hands with your clients, but the point is the same. *Never* let the client even *imagine* that you have lost touch with them. You need to keep in constant verbal contact with them. You need to dance with them (symbolically), shifting focus and questions in accordance to their reactions and perspectives. Remember that the truly trusted guide is tethered to her client. How foolish would it be for a guide to fail to stay in visual and verbal contact with a person to whom she is tethered?

The Discuss phase of the 3D coaching model must stay a discussion. It is not a lecture, it is not a pitch, and it is not a chance to manipulate your prospect. Rather, it is a chance to co-create something of great value for the prospect that serves you because you make money and you have impact!

How this phase differentiates the consultative sales professional from the coach

Remember our discussion of get, give, and guide? We compared consultative selling and the coaching model using these terms, where consultative selling is like get/give and coaching is better represented by the principle of guide. In the discussion phase of the 3D coaching model, the comparison is as follows:

- Get/Give can be like a tug-of-war battle or ping-pong match
- Get/Give often focuses on manipulation to move the person to your side
- Get/Give uses the trial close and will be seen by the knowledgeable client
- Guiding is like a dance where it is hard to know where one's movement begins and ends
- Strong guides stay completely connected with clients—like if climbing a mountain, the person is out of breath and has to stop. What would happen if the guide kept going up the mountain? He would lose the client!
- Guide works on the collaborative close model

Discussion, collaboration, and teamwork will help you form advocates and partners. It will help you be seen as a valuable coach rather than a vendor who could be quickly replaced. Which identity feels better to you?

Work through Blocks to Achieving Goals

We mentioned earlier that a coach helps clients strategize solutions. If you find your prospect is wishy-washy or hesitant during the Discuss phase, then you must focus on an additional coaching skill: helping prospects work through blocks (which you might know as objections) to decide on a purchase. In a coaching situation, you will always run into blocks for clients achieving what they want. Part of the coaching relationship is the understanding that the coach is there to help the individual work through these blocks and reach their goals. Is it really all that different in a sales situation? Many times, the prospect is blocked by some perception or fact and the sales professional could do them an invaluable service by helping them overcome that block.

So what does a skilled coach do when the client is showing mixed motivations or hesitancies? One technique is to build a pain/pleasure chart. While this is completely based on the work of psychologists around reinforcement theory, we first stumbled across these terms used in *Awaken the Giant Within* by Anthony Robbins.

By looking at pain and pleasure, you can determine what behavior or decision a person will make. You can also reveal blocks that are keeping a person from making a decision. However, it is somewhat deceiving to say that pain and pleasure determine this. More accurately, it is the *perception* of pain and pleasure that will dictate action. If I truly believe that one decision will result in pleasure and the other will result in pain, unless I am a masochist, I will pursue the decision that will give me the least pain and most pleasure.

Let's take an example in a sales situation where a person is trying to decide whether or not to buy a new expensive home. The cost is above what she had been planning to spend, but she is in love with the house. A sales professional skilled in the coaching process could take her through a series of questions to help reveal the perceived pain and pleasure. Some we have trained actually use a chart to do this. They basically list the two decisions that the person could make and then fill in the pain and pleasure of each decision as shown below. Below is a blank version of this:

	Pain of doing it	Pleasure of doing it
Option #1		
Option #2		

Now let's apply this format to the person deciding on the home purchase. By asking her about each of the categories of pain and pleasure, the real estate professional has now gathered the following information:

	Pain	Pleasure
Option #1: Buying the house	• It is more than I budgeted for • May not be able to go on as many vacations due to finances • Feel like I am being financially irresponsible	• This is really the house of my dreams • I would finally have the space that I have always wanted • I could entertain friends well in this house
Option #2: Not buying the house	• I haven't been able to find anything else that I like as much • This may be my best choice and I could blow it • I could be stuck in the house I currently have and hate for a longer time	• I would have more money each month for other things • I might find something I like for a lesser price • I get to avoid making a potentially uncomfortable decision

Would this be useful information in the discussion phase for the sales professional? Absolutely! With this information, the sales professional could walk the buyer through different options and thoughts to help clarify the right buying decision for the person. For example, he might problem solve some of the pain of buying the house by comparing the value of different types of infrequent vacations with the value of daily comfort. He builds a vision of the pleasure of owning the home and entertaining friends that would help the buyer feel more confident about the purchase. He might look at the realities of her budget and see what is best for her. However, without this information, the selling professional is helpless to really help her walk through solutions. By looking at the perceived pain and pleasure, the professional can impact her decision in a way that (if ethically done) will greatly aid the client and build a raving fan.

A Coaching Tool: Storyboarding

Storyboarding is a helpful technique for uncovering your natural wisdom about your products and services. It is especially helpful when you have a lot of "mind traffic" and need to organize your thoughts and strategize approaches. While storyboarding can be used for any process (such as writing a book, determining a marketing plan, working through complex problems, etc.), for our purposes we are going to use it to help come up with your three-point play. We will describe the steps here. You will be asked to actually do this in the exercise section of this chapter. In order to do the exercise, all you need are sticky notes and a medium thick felt pen. This exercise can be done alone or with a sales team.

The suggested steps to the storyboarding technique are as follows:
- Identify
- Cluster
- Label

Identify

The first step of the storyboarding process requires that you leave all judgment at the door. There is no place for criticism, processing, distraction, or details in the brainstorming process. For this phase to work most successfully, you simply start brainstorming all of the different strengths of your product or service. As you say these aloud, write one idea down per sticky note and plaster it on the wall. Just think about everything you might want to tell a prospect about your product. Keep writing down one idea per sheet of sticky notes until you have exhausted all of your ideas.

Cluster

Next, start moving your notes around. Cluster or "chunk" similar themes together. Which sticky notes seem related in some way? Do this by instinct, and keep moving them around until you have formed three categories of notes. Discard any repetitive notes and any notes that do not fit into these three categories. If they do not fit, then they are likely "noise" that will just interfere with your presentation. If you notice that any ideas are missing, then simply grab a sticky note and add them. Step back and look at your categories, continuing to play with them until you are satisfied.

Label

Look at each of the three clusters of notes. What theme brings them together? For example, if you have clustered several notes together that say, "not complex," "high client satisfaction rate," "user friendly," and "simplistic design," the category might be captured by the phrase "easy to use."

Write your category name on another sticky note in a different color and place the category name above the grouping of phrases.

After you have done these three steps, you are able to build a three-point play sheet that lists these top strengths and write out the nuances that come from the notes below the main category. Put this on a couple of index cards or a single sheet of paper as a reminder of these strengths.

This simple act of organizing your thoughts into a powerful three-point play will help you be laser focused in your sales meetings and more prepared to truly coach the sale. We hope this process makes sense to you. However, it will really come alive when you do it, so let's move on to putting this into practice.

EXERCISE: Storyboarding

Now that we have described storyboarding for you, let's actually do it. Think about your product or service and follow these steps:

Identify
Without criticism or discussion, brainstorm the strengths of your product or service. Put one down per sticky note and plaster them to the wall.

Cluster
When all ideas are exhausted, start clustering similar themes until you are satisfied with your chunks of information. Create three main clusters with your sticky notes. Put aside anything that does not fit into these three main categories. Add any additional ideas to the three categories that come to mind.

Label
Label your three categories using a different color pen and place the category name above the grouping of phrases. Use these strengths in the next exercise to create your three-point play.

EXERCISE: The Three-Point Play

The point of this exercise is to help you master the three-point play. By completing this, you will focus on the most important things about your product/services and create your own concise story. Basically, you are creating three succinct reasons why someone should buy from you, supported with compelling facts and benefits. Be sure that your benefits answer the "What is in it for me?" question that your prospect will be asking him or herself. It is best to do this exercise for each product or service that you provide. While walking through this will be mechanical, once you have mastered the approach, you will be able to choose the words that are most genuine to your personality and approach. We are going to work with you in this section to create a single three-point play. However, for those of you who are really ambitious, you can try to create your three-point play differently for each of the four different T.E.A.M. styles presented in the last chapter.

Use the following formula to create a three-point play. To do this, you will have to either role-play with a colleague or recall a recent prospect interaction. Use the example found previously in this chapter to help form this.

Share point #1: One of the greatest advantages of...

_____

_____

Connect it back to the initial goals:
I know that you mentioned...

_____

_____

_____

Check in with the prospect with a question:
How does the idea of...

_____

_____

_____

Pause

So it sounds like we are in agreement that...

_____

_____

_____

Is that right?

Share point #2: Another thing that I think you
will find intriguing is that...

_____

_____

_____

Connect it back to the initial goals: I hope that you
can see that I am really trying to address the goals
that you shared at the beginning of our conversation. I know you mentioned that you would like to...

_____

_____

Check in with the prospect with a question:
What would be your vision for...

_____

_____

_____

Pause

After sharing, pause and come to agreement on how
your service meets the goal. Then move on to point
three of the three-point play.

Share point #3:
The third thing that I believe you might be
interested in is...

_____

_____

_____

Connect it back to the initial goals: I know that
you have...

_____

_____

_____

Check in with the prospect with a question:
What questions do you have about...

_____

_____

_____

Now practice this formula with a friend or colleague. Find a pace and style that fits for you and
feels genuine in approach and style.

EXERCISE: The Reflective Review

Bring to mind your last sales meeting. To the best of your ability, try to form a reflective review in hindsight. Use the following formula:

It sounds like we are in agreement on...

_____

(Name play #1: Your first solution)

_____

(Name play #2: Your second solution)

_____

(Name play #3: Your third solution)

...matching up well with...

_____

(Name client goal or goals)

If you are unable to do this, what does that suggest? How will you improve your ability to do the reflective review?

Chapter 5

The Coaching Model Phase 3:

Decide

"The time to stop talking is when the other person
nods his head affirmatively but says nothing."
—Anonymous

"Live in such a way that you would not be ashamed to
sell your parrot to the town gossip."
—Will Rogers

Overview

A talented coach helps move a prospect to actions and solutions. Now that you and your prospect have discovered the goals and issues and have discussed solutions, it is time to move the meeting to some form of accountability. Less experienced sales professionals do their prospects a disservice by failing to guide the conversation to a decision. While a full purchasing decision is not always possible in the moment, some decision that will move the sales process ahead is *always* possible. In this chapter, you will learn how to do a collaborative close, form meaningful action steps, and develop solid time lines with clients for follow up. Also, we will look at a formula using a coaching style for handling objections during the critical-yard conversation.

Tales from the Playing Field

I was young and not particularly well off when I needed to buy a car for basic transportation. I was walking around the dealership when the sales professional came up to me to "help" me with my decision. He was gregarious and energetic and started telling me about all of the great features of the new Cadillac that we happened to be standing in front of. After about ten minutes, I interrupted him and told him that I was looking for a used car. Here is how the dialogue proceeded from there.

> Salesperson: So, here is a nice car for only thirteen thousand and five hundred dollars. What is great about this car is blah, blah, blah.
>
> Me: Actually, I wasn't planning on spending that much.
>
> Salesperson: Well, over here we have a decent ride for only eleven thousand and nine hundred

dollars. What you will love about this fine piece of machinery is blah, blah, blah.

Me: I hate to interrupt you, but it is still out of my price range.

Salesperson: Well good night, how much are you planning on spending?

Me: I have about twenty-five hundred dollars.

Salesperson: Oh, you want a *#!* box! We keep those around back.

Me: Thanks for your time.

I didn't buy from this gentleman and obviously he was not very helpful in terms of aiding me to make a decision!

Principles

We "get" sales professionals. Therefore, we know that many of you reading this book have skipped to this Decide chapter first. If you are one of them, then turn the pages back to the beginning and read it in order; it will serve you best! If you have had the patience to explore the first several phases of this model, then everything is about to pay off.

Understandably, sales professionals focus on getting the prospect to decide so that they can close the sale. Most closings in a sales situation are manipulative. If the first two stages of the 3D model have been followed, then ours is not manipulative, but it is a "gimme." Or to continue with our critical-yard theme, at this stage you have run your ninety-five yards and now you can just waltz in on that last five yards. The goal of this phase is to get a "yes" or to fully understand and support a "no."

Some of our coaching colleagues have difficulty in selling coaching. They have an illusion that trying to close a deal is disrespectful in some ways to their prospect. Truthfully, the most talented coaches know that accountability is a great gift to give to your client.

Let's revisit the skills of a coach. Coaches aid a client to move conversation to action/solution. Some people make the mistake of seeing coaching as a somewhat "fluffy" profession that is all about making the person feel good. While bringing out the strengths and confidence of the client is a crucial part of the coaching process, the focus is not just on feeling good or happy. Rather, coaching is about transformation. It is about seeing your goals and reaching them. It is about living at your potential and following your mission. Therefore, all coaching interactions (at least the ones we do) end with action. The actions cho-

sen are often picked by the person being coached, but they are often co-created with the coach. These actions are focused on behaviors that will take the client to his or her next level of happiness and performance. Coaching without action is simply *not* coaching.

In a sales situation, there must be action at the end of the interaction. The prospect must make one of the following choices:

✓ Buy
✓ Don't buy
✓ Postpone the decision

Each of these decisions will result in action steps needed. For example, a buy decision will lead to action around signing a contract, handing over money, and so on. A "don't buy" decision will dictate the actions of the sales professional. Many times, the professional needs to accept the "no" and focus on more promising prospects. The "postpone the decision" is the one where the next action may not be readily apparent, but is important to reveal. If a prospect decides to postpone the decision, the two worst things that the sales professional can do (if following a coaching model) are to push the client to a decision or completely leave the decision alone without having action steps to help the person move to a decision.

Accountability Is Important

Accountability is an important part of a coaching relationship. However, for some, accountability is a scary word. To be accountable means simply that–to give an account. Accountability is about taking responsibility for your successes, decisions, and life, and learning from all challenges. Accountability can be a very vulnerable experience for the client, but can also be very empowering if handled with empathy, respect, and strength. Coaches can limit the success of your client by creating a sense of shame and judgment. However, they can also limit the success of their client by "letting them off the hook" too easily. Both are disrespectful to the client.

Sample accountability questions in a coaching relationship include:
- What will you do?
- When will you do it? (For how long)
- How will I know you've done it?

So how does this apply in a sales situation? Even when the client is not ready to make a decision, the professional who is coaching the sale needs to help him or her form action steps that will help the individual move closer to the decision. If the prospect isn't sure if he wants to hire you as his financial advisor, then what does he need to learn, do, or explore in order to make a decision? What actions does he need to take to help himself move from a state of indecision and also not waste your time? These are questions that need to be tactfully poised to the prospect, out of care for both the individual and for your own time and energy. The prospect needs to feel from you that it is okay if he doesn't know his decision yet, but that it is in both of your best interests to find ways to move closer to a decision.

Talented sales professionals are not hesitant to call a prospect to accountability in a respectful and yet truthful way. They know that it serves all involved to make a decision. They also respect the prospect's timing in that decision and are not threatened if the decision is not to buy from them. True sales professionals believe in abundance and know that moving people to decisions, even if the decision is a "no," is good for their careers and for their bottom line.

The Decide phase of the 3D critical yard model is likely the easiest to execute. In fact, this is the shortest chapter because all the work has been done at this point and the decision should not be much of an issue. You have been clarifying issues and doing "trial closes" throughout the last two phases. Your main goal in this phase is to be as specific as possible when you aid the prospect to move to action.

Coaching vs. Traditional Sales

The similarities between the Decide phase of the coaching the sale model and traditional sales approaches:

- Both lead to getting a yes, no, or maybe decision from the prospect
- Both are an attempt to close the sale
- Both desire concrete results

The differences between the Decide phase of the coaching conversation and traditional sales approaches:

- The level of collaboration between sales professional and prospect
- The level of letting the prospect self-discover his or her best decision
- The amount of energy expenditure required of the sales professional

Let's take a look at each of these more closely.

The Level of Collaboration

The model for this stage of the coaching conversation centers around the collaboration and accountability. In a traditional sales approach and even a consultative selling situation, you do what is called the trial close. During the trial close, you are determining whether or not the prospect is ready to buy, and you try to move him or her to a buying decision. In the coaching model for sales, you are providing an opportunity for the prospect to close herself in a way that serves her best and also accomplishes your need to know when to celebrate a sale, revisit the issues, or move on to the next prospect. Some coaching purists may have a problem with this until they realize that accountability and helping a client move to a measurable action step is part of most major coach training programs. The only difference in applying this to a sales situation is that you, the sales professional, benefit from the client deciding to purchase your product or service. The element that makes this feasible in our opinion is integrity. If the sales professional is operating with integrity, then the answer that the client gets to will truly be the one that is right for her. If the sales professional is not going to act with integrity, well, we doubt very much that they would be interested in the approach that we are taking with this book. There are easier and better ways to manipulate people if that is your goal. Within our model, there is constant co-creation of the results of the meeting.

The Level of Letting the Prospect Self-Discover His or Her Best Decision

While this concept might sound odd to some sales professionals, we believe that the most solid and profitable decisions are those that you guide the prospect to without pushing it upon him. Your prospects are experts in one thing that you can never be an expert in. They know better than you do what is best for their life. As coaches, your authors believe that we have a lot to offer our clients. We have techniques, information, and skills that we truly feel will benefit our clients. However, we are not arrogant enough to believe that what we offer is best for everyone. People and their needs are too unique for that to be true. A skilled coach has the humility to know that there is a lot that he does not know. Your prospect has to live with the consequences of the buying decision. A professional following the coaching the sale model wants the client to have a level of accountability and determination that only comes when he discovers the decision to buy.

So what does this really mean? Obviously, we have supported the idea of sharing the benefits of your product and services, so we are not asking you to be passive. Rather, we are just promoting that once you have guided them to the matching of your products and their needs, you back off from trying to convince them of buying what you have to offer.

For example, an older sales technique is something called the assumed close. In the assumed close, you ask a question that is based on an assumption that the individual has already decided to buy the service or product. Let's say that you have been trying to sell your coaching services to a client. The assumed close would be something like:

- So when did you want to start your coaching with me?
- I have next Tuesday morning free for us to get started working on our coaching; is that free for you?
- I know that this coaching relationship is going to work great for you, and I can't wait to get started.

This technique of the assumed close used to be effective with a certain type of prospect. However, as we stated at the beginning of this book, you are now dealing with a much more sophisticated and skeptical buyer. They don't want to feel coerced into the purchase, and when they sense manipulation, they push back or disappear. Maybe the time has come for a much more respectful style. Some examples of a coaching the sale approach at the same point in the conversation are:

- So what would you like to do about coaching together?
- What else can we talk about to help you make a decision about your choice of coaches?
- I would really enjoy working with you and hope you feel the same. However, the most important thing is you connecting with a coach that matches best for you. If you feel comfortable discussing it, how are you feeling about the match between us?
- What do you need to make a decision about your coaching?

You will notice that these questions still work to move someone to a buying decision (which we strongly support). If you value your time and believe in your product or service, then you will not be shy about helping the prospect move to decide about it. Indecisiveness does not serve anyone involved.

The Amount of Energy Expenditure Required of the Sales Professional

Manipulation and persuasion, especially with a resistant prospect, can be huge energy drainers. One great fringe benefit of the 3D coaching model and the coaching the sale process is that it does not tend to trigger any resistance. When done well, it is like having a good conversation with a friend that is solution-focused and caring. We find that when sales professionals use this model, they feel energized, even when they don't get the sale. Once coaching the sale becomes second nature to you, the experience of truly trying to aid the client will feel great.

How secure are you in your success as a sale professional? Do you have a spirit of abundance (the sales are out there—you will get many because they are unlimited) or do you tend to fear rejection and exhausting possible prospects? To follow the coaching the sale model, you must be a believer in abundance. You must make a choice about your beliefs, deciding that if you follow the process, you will do fine. Fear has no place in this model. Fear only drains energy. Confidence allows you to stick to the process and do the right thing. And in our experience, that is when the finances tend to take care of themselves. By following the model, you can live each day energized by the way you are treating people and living your life. Then when those sales happen (and they will), this energy will simply go through the roof. So let's look at the model that will allow you to do this in the Decide phase of the 3D model.

The Model for Deciding

The model for guiding a prospect through the Decide phase of the coaching conversation is captured by the acronym CAT. This is a simple process with three parts made up of the following:

- Collaborative close—a style for seeing if a decision has been made
- Action steps—guiding the prospect to form firm commitments

• Timing and follow up–forming an accountability plan to ensure movement and progress in the process

Collaborative Close

The collaborative close is a way to determine the prospect's buying decision, while potentially uncovering any blocks keeping you from forming a mutually beneficial relationship with the prospect. As with most of the coaching process, the collaborative close is based more on questions than statements. We gave you some examples of this already in our coaching example. Additional general examples of starting the collaborative close are:

✓ Given what we have discussed, what makes sense to you at this point?

✓ So what are your thoughts after walking through your goals and the ideas we discussed for solutions?

✓ I hope that you have been able to tell that I really want you to make the right decision for yourself here. What makes sense as the next step to you?

If you get a "no" or "no decision," you have the choice to accept it (realizing that your product or service is not in the prospect's best interests) or to move back to the Discover phase of the discussion. You would choose to move back to the Discover phase if you feel that the "no" or "no decision" is due to you missing something in the coaching process (or when you want to learn from the interaction). An example approach to returning back to the discover phase is:

• Obviously I missed something and I really want to understand your view on this. What is holding you back from moving ahead with this?

There are many reasons why, despite your belief that your product or service is best for the prospect, he may decide otherwise or be indecisive. We have built a chart of possible answers to the question, "What is holding you back from making this purchase?" connected with potential follow-up coaching questions you might ask.

Potential answer to "What is holding you back from making this purchase?"	Potential follow-up coaching question
The price is too high	*If we were able to agree on a price and money wasn't an issue, what else would hold you back?*
Time	*How might you go about problem-solving the time issue?*
My spouse	*What can I do to help the two of you get on the same page with this?*
Just can't decide yet	*What is your main concern about making a decision?*
I told another salesperson I would meet with him before deciding	*How would you feel about giving me a chance to discuss it with you after you meet with him?*
I really want to switch to you, but I feel loyal to the current person providing this service	*What are some other ways to be loyal to this person that still allow you to pursue the service that is best for you?*

Each of you readers will have to decide how comfortable you are with these follow-up questions. However, the point of them is not to coerce your prospect. Rather, they are meant to serve your prospect to help him make sure he makes the absolute best decision for himself.

Could they be misused for selfish gain? Of course! But that is where you will need to check your philosophy and your heart. You are the only one who can judge that. However, on the other end of the continuum are people with misguided integrity that somehow have come to the belief that wanting to make a profit is wrong. We believe that a win-win is often possible as long as you truly address the blocks your prospect has and don't just try to manipulate your way around them. But when you do not challenge their blocks, you may be leaving the prospect open to the next sales professional that may not approach the task with the same level of integrity and may manipulate the person to a poor buying decision. These coaching questions will get the blocks on the table so you can aid your prospect to make a conscious and wise decision.

Indifference, Skepticism, and True Drawback

There are three major reasons that a prospect would say "no" to you or hesitate to make a decision. He is either indifferent, skeptical, or there is a true drawback for him to follow your solution. The "no" is going to be either factual or emotional. If he is indifferent, then it is highly likely that you have failed to follow our 3D model. If you had followed the model well, then you would understand what emotion is driving his buying decision and you would have drawn this out of the prospect. If your prospect is indifferent, then start the model over again and follow it more closely (if he will even allow it at this point).

If the prospect is skeptical, then some fear is creeping in for him. Your job in this case is to be caring enough to help him overcome the fear. Take the time to acknowledge and reveal his concerns. Problem solve with the prospect ways to buy, but still address the potential fears. For example, what if you are trying to sell a service to someone who already gets that service from a friend? The prospect sees it as disloyal to his friend to work with you. Many sales rookies try to argue with the prospect, telling him to separate friendship from business (which, of course, fails). Your goal in our model is to try to explore ways that the prospect could stay loyal to his friend and *still* do business with you. Don't go up against his value; rather, work with the person to problem-solve different ways to look at the situation. This requires creative, out-of-the-box thinking on both of your parts.

Finally, if there is a true drawback to him buying your product or service, then your job is to help him feel comfortable with that decision. Show a true and genuine care by acknowledging that it is a "square peg in a round hole," that neither of you has done something wrong, but it is not a good fit. Emphasize that you were not meeting with him just to make a sale–you were meeting with him to aid him to make the best purchasing decision. Of course, after this discussion might be a good time to ask him for referrals for your business before you part ways! Remember the story from earlier in the book about the financial planner who discouraged me from purchasing one of his products? He has made ten times more in referrals from me than he would have made from forcing a sale on me. Keep your integrity in the process, believe in abundance, and you will be more successful.

The Importance of Your Nonverbal Stance

One way to determine if your integrity or your selfishness is leading you is to watch your nonverbal patterns. If you are truly looking out for your prospect's best decision, then you will be energetic, peaceful, engaged, thoughtful, and patient. If selfishness is involved, you will show frustration, impatience, pressured speech, and desire for control. Just doing a quick check in on your body can help give you insight into what is going on for you. Just ask yourself, "How does my body feel right now?" and "What am I showing to my prospect with my nonverbal behaviors?"

So let's walk through a specific example of this. You are a financial advisor and you have just met with a high net worth prospect. You feel like you have walked through the coaching process well, but at the end of the meeting, the person says that she doesn't know what decision she wants to make. You sense that it has to do with your fee structure and you want to reveal that in the meeting so that you can address the obstacle. Here is a sample conversation with that prospect that demonstrates coaching her to a decision:

> Advisor: Obviously I missed something and I really want to understand your view on this. What is holding you back from moving ahead with this?
>
> Prospect: I'm just not sure I like your fee policy. I am familiar with paying only when I do transactions.
>
> Advisor: Okay, well I certainly want you to feel comfortable with my approach; what specifically causes you concern about the fee policy?
>
> Prospect: I'm just not sure it makes sense for me financially. I mean, you could just be draining my finances without really doing anything for me.

Advisor: I appreciate your honesty and agree that any advisor that would drain you without providing a service is someone to stay away from. Do you know what benefits you might see in a fee arrangement?

Prospect: Well, I have never done it, so obviously I haven't seen the benefit.

Advisor: That certainly makes sense. I know one thing that I tell my clients, and that I fully believe, is that a fee arrangement puts the two of us on the same side of the table. We are closer partners with your money. When you make less money, I make less money. What impact do you think this makes on me?

Prospect: Well, I know you guys like money, so it would tend to motivate you to keep my portfolio progressing.

Advisor: Absolutely! Given that arrangement, what motivation would I have to take my eyes off your money and let it dwindle?

Prospect: None that I can think of.

Advisor: Now compare that with someone who gets paid every time they put in an order for you. They get the same whether you make money or not. Which relationship do you think would be more proactive about making sure you are making money?

Prospect: I see your point.

Advisor: Well, I do want you to see my point, but more importantly, I want you to be at complete peace with whatever decision you make here. What else do we need to discuss to help you decide?

If the advisor had never coached out the prospect's concerns, then he would have definitely lost the sale. While coaching does not guarantee the sale 100 percent of the time, just think of the impact if it could increase your sales results even a minimal of 10–20 percent!

Action Steps—What Are the Next Steps?

The next several stages of the CAT process are simplistic. In the case the decision is "yes," they want your services, we assume that you know exactly what to do. Whenever you get a prospect's decision or statement of no decision, you always want to form next steps and move the prospect to action.

If the decision is "no," then most sales professionals either write off the prospect or ask a question such as, "How would you feel if I checked in with you in the future to see if your needs are different?" There is a better way to handle this type of situation. If the prospect is indecisive, there are several potential coaching questions to move to action steps:

- When would be a time to check in with you again?
- What will you do in the meantime to help advance your decision?
- How can I aid you in deciding?
- How would you feel about setting up an appointment to go over the issues again once you have had a chance to think this through? How about a week from today to do that?

Then we encourage you to put a note in your PDA or calendar to trigger your follow up. Poor follow through is death for a sales professional, and we have seen too many individuals destroy a great sale due to poor follow up. Whatever systems works for you is fine. Just make sure you have a system that ensures the action steps are completed.

Timing and Follow Up—When Should We Check In Again to See Our Progress?

This last stage of the CAT process will differ depending on your industry and your support from the home office. If others do the follow up for you, then this may not apply. However, for the rest of us, we must remember that timing and follow up is an important stage in the selling process. Even if the contract is signed, if you want to turn customers into advocates, one of the best ways is to check in with them during the follow-up process with simple questions like:

- How is everything working?
- What could I do for you that I haven't done yet?
- When would you like to check in again for future needs?

So in the CAT process, you walk through a collaborative close, form action steps, and determine timing and follow up. With this process, you will guide the prospect through the Decide phase of our 3D model and lead him or her to their best buying decision. During this process, you may encounter hesitancies or verbal challenges from your prospect. So let's examine a coaching tool for dealing with prospect objections.

Coaching Tool: APPA

Our final coaching tool for the 3D model of coaching the sale is APPA. This stands for:

- **A**cknowledge
- **P**ursue
- **P**rovide
- **A**cceptance

APPA is a conversational structure that aids the sales professional with dealing with objections from the prospect.

It is a simple structure that is easy to remember and easy to execute when the prospect has objections, questions, or doubts. Remember the three concerns of indifference, skepticism, and true drawback? This is the process to use when you are attempting to cross the critical yard with a skeptical prospect, but you are certain that your product or service will serve him or her well.

Acknowledge

Rookie salespersons respond to objections with a defensive stance and tend to fight their clients. Skilled professionals show understanding in the face of objections. They acknowledge the fears and potential pains and "normalize" the prospect's remarks in order to diffuse the tension in the interaction. Acknowledging is simply reflecting back the prospect's objecting nondefensively and in a way that shows that you really do understand his hesitancy. For example, "It sounds like you are concerned about the length of this contract—that is understandable and it is a good thing for us to look at together to make sure this is right for you."

Pursue

After acknowledging the prospect's emotions, you simply do a mini Discover phase by pursuing the concerns. Ask the prospect powerful questions to determine the *real* objections that he or she is having. Questions like, "Tell me what it is about _____ that concerns you" can help the person self-discover the blocks that did not pop up earlier in the process. By helping him go deeper with a safe and respectful style, you will get to the main blocks.

Provide

Once you have discovered the blocks, it is time to provide the prospect with solutions. Work together with the individual to provide answers to the issues or to look at the issue in a different way. For example, when we have clients who have concerns about price, we will often help them turn their attention from the exact dollars to the value that they are getting for the dollars spent. Keep this interaction to the same style as you had in the discussion phase of this model.

Acceptance

Coaches end conversations with action, so work with the prospect to co-create a specific action step. If you have dealt with his objection well, then he will feel a level of acceptance about the buying decision. Ask questions like, "Have I sufficiently dealt with your concern?" to make sure there are no other blocks. Then finish the Decide phase of the model with concrete next steps.

By using this simple model, you will deal with any objections that impact the buying decision. If buying your service or product is truly best for him, then you will have removed any false blocks and will likely make the sale.

EXERCISE: Handling "No" or Hesitancy to Decide

Answer the following questions to help grow your abilities in the Decide phase of the 3D coaching model:

Write down several examples from recent attempts at selling where you receive a "no" or "no decision":

_____

_____

How might you deal with that situation differently now using a coaching approach?

_____

_____

What could you still do to recapture the possibility of making that sale?

_____

_____

How can you use this information in the future (and how will you discipline yourself to remember and practice it)?

_____

_____

_____

EXERCISE: The Collaborative Close

Create your own collaborative close questions. Do two of these starting with the word "what" and two starting with the word "how":

What...

_____

_____

_____

What...

_____

_____

_____

How...

_____

_____

_____

How...

_____

_____

_____

EXERCISE: Your Nonverbal Communication

Practice your communication in front of a mirror (if you work on the phone, you can benefit from this too). However, instead of just practicing your smile, etc., we want you to watch yourself ask coaching questions around the collaborative close, moving to action, or timing and follow through. As you do this, answer the following questions.

What do I really like about how I present myself?

_____

_____

_____

What would I like to do differently or better?

_____

_____

_____

To what degree is the real me coming out? How genuine do I look and how might I show who I am even more in this process?

_____

_____

_____

Section III

Transforming to the Next Level

Chapter 6

Confidence:

The Fuel for Tomorrow's Success

"No matter how brilliant a man may be, he will never engender confidence in his subordinates and associates if he lacks simple honesty and moral courage."
—J. Lawton Collins

"I am the greatest. I said that even before I knew I was. "
—Muhammad Ali

Overview

To truly make the transformation to someone who masters the critical yard and coaches the sale, you must have great confidence. Self-confidence is the fuel for the effective sales professional. Handling challenges all day, staying persistent in the face of the all-powerful "no," and continuing to find creative ways to deal with prospects can take their toll on even the most skilled professional. To take a coaching approach to sales means you must be living as confidently as possible. In this chapter, we will explore five different approaches to building the most confident you.

Tales from the Playing Field

It was a big-ticket sale and one that I wanted badly. This was my second interview with the prospect group and they wanted a six-month extensive program on communication, confidence, and coaching skills. They were looking at my group to develop the training and provide all of the follow-up coaching to their key employees. It was a wonderful opportunity. I was meeting with the CEO, COO, the director of sales, and the HR director, and they were all strong and potentially intimidating individuals. I was outnumbered and their questions were flying at me left and right. With intense tones and looks, they were firing questions at me like:

- How will we know for sure that we will get results?
- What kind of guarantee do you give to your work?
- Why should we hire you above the other three people we are looking at, especially since you are more expensive?

Despite my training, there is still a tendency to want to decrease my fee to get engagements of this size. However, I know better than to take that scarcity mentality. So before I answered their questions, I had to answer them for myself:

- Do I believe 100 percent that they will get results?
- What kind of guarantee am I willing to give them?
- Why should they hire me if there are less expensive providers available to them?

My answers to myself were crucial:

- My clients who work the program always get results. So as long as they work it, I *completely* believe they will get results. I know that this stuff works!

- If I don't help them (which is not going to be the case) then I don't want their money, so I'll guarantee them results as long as they do their part in the program—I have no problem with that!
- Why should they hire me if there are less expensive providers available to them? Well, with the other providers they are taking their chances—some might be decent and some might be lousy. I *know* that I can aid them; I have no idea if the others can, so I'm not going to risk that for my client!

Only after quickly assessing these answers in my head could I confidently relay the information to my clients. Of course, I continued to use a coaching model and tied back into their perspectives and desires. But I left no doubt in their minds that I could do the job. I did not do this with arrogance, but I did share the information with strength and certainty.

After the job was completed, we moved to a very nice retainer relationship and have been working together for years. I asked the CEO at the end of that first big job why they picked me over the other coaches they were interviewing. He said that the only reason they chose me over the other providers was because the others squirmed at the three questions about results, guarantee, and price. He looked at me straight in the eyes and said, "We needed someone who really knew what he was doing. We chose you because of your confidence."

Principles

It would be crazy for us to think that we can drive our cars without the appropriate fuel. Most of us see the empty light come on when it is time to get more gas. Are you responding to your empty light?

In a competitive environment between two sales professionals of similar skill level, self-confidence will determine who succeeds in crossing the critical yard and who does not. The one with the low fuel tank will walk away more depleted while the one who took the time to fill her tank will walk away more energized (and profitable).

Do you have an early warning light when your energy is getting too low and you need to recharge? Many of us avoid listening to our bodies until we experience burnout, exhaustion, or sometimes even physical symptoms. If we wait until we are depleted before recharging, then it takes much more time and energy to fill ourselves up than if we had addressed it immediately.

Building Your Confidence (Even If You Are Already a Confident Person)

But forget about waiting until we need a recharge! What is the value of building your confidence at all times? The value is that you will have the means necessary to outplay the competition!

Have you ever watched a sports game live or on television and seen the impact of confidence? History has shown that a team of lower skill can defeat a team of greater skill if their confidence is significantly higher. In business, many times the promotion will go to the person who exudes the most confidence, even if he or she is not the highest-qualified person. In sales, confidence is even more critical. The sales professional who has the most confidence will often walk out the winner in a competitive bidding situation, even if her product is not necessarily the best. And the opposite is true also. You may have the best product in the world, but if you approach your prospect with low confidence, then you may kill the sale. Clients want confidence in the person consulting them. They can sniff out insecurity and will run for the hills from the stench.

Take a natural athlete who has all of the innate abilities, but doesn't succeed. What is it that determines her prowess? If her performance was based completely on raw talent or ability, then she would have gone on to be one of the greats. But take a great athlete and give her only average confidence and you will get a good performer who is always one critical yard away from being great.

To coach the sale, you must become unconsciously competent. You want automatic confidence that comes from:

• Knowledge
• Skills
• Habit

The traditional sales professional knows the importance of *knowledge* of your product and your field. We do not disagree with this at all! To have your top level of confidence, you must be educated on your prospects and the features and benefits of your product. A top sales professional must also have the *skills* necessary to sell. You must be a great listener, a persuasive speaker, and a good relater, and have the ability to problem-solve. Finally, you want to create the *habit* of success, which requires practicing the behaviors that will make you successful. That is why we have built this book with exercises. Having the knowledge of how to coach is not going to improve your game. Practicing this knowledge, building the skills, and making these habitual will take your game to the next level.

Why Someone Coaching the Sale Must Be Unusually Confident

So is confidence really that important for a sales professional who wants to coach the sale? Face it, few professions meet with the same level of adversity as sales. Few people get rejected as much or have to deal with disrespectful prospects. Some people give themselves permission to be rude to sales professionals (although many individuals in sales have brought that on themselves).

A career in sales is not for the timid, and has challenges every day that must be faced with strength and confidence. A sales professional who has lost his confidence cannot make a living. Your job security and level of success depends on the level of your confidence. You simply cannot be in sales if you lack confidence.

Even those with decent levels of confidence can lose a sale to a competitor who shows more confidence. Let's go back to our guide example. Let's imagine that you are about to embark on a challenging climb up a dangerous mountain peak (it is not dissimilar to how prospects feel before shelling out a lot of money). Which guide would you prefer?

- One who was insecure about his ability to lead you up the mountain ("I'm not going to kid you, this is one rough trip, and I've only done a few, so don't expect it to go perfectly.")
- One who showed an average level of confidence in his knowledge and ability to make the trip work for you ("I

think I am the right guide for you and hope it will be a good trip; they usually go fine.")

- One who showed incredible confidence in his ability to make the trip successful and specific to your goals (I've done this hundreds of times and it will not only be safe, but you are going to have the experience of your life.")

I doubt any of us would tether ourselves to the first guide. We *might* consider tethering ourselves to the second guide; however, we would quickly drop him if the third guide was present. It wouldn't even be a contest!

But remember, a "confident" coach who shows no interest or care for her client's perspectives and needs is often seen as arrogant. A confident coach who shows great care for understanding and aiding her client is seen as a valued partner. Confidence builds trust, trust builds relationships, and relationships build success for all involved. Prospects will follow a sales professional who they trust will be a confident and capable guide to the right purchasing decision.

Five Paths to Confidence

Are you an *inspirational* coach? If not, then this section can help you transform! Are you inspirational, but know you can be even better? Then this section can help tweak your confidence and bring it up to the next level. So let's get started on doing that.

Most confidence books focus on self-talk strategies to build confidence. While these strategies can be highly effective, they are not complete in and of themselves. To work on your thinking alone is like going to the gym and just working on your biceps. Your biceps may look great, but your abs, quads, triceps, or pecs may get neglected, and therefore your body isn't nearly as magnificent as it could be. In regards to confidence, the parallel of a full-circuit gym comes from working out strategies in the following five areas:

- Mental (thinking approaches)
- Emotional (feeling approaches)
- Behavioral (action-oriented approaches)
- Relational (community approaches)
- Spiritual (life purpose and mission approaches)

These strategies are covered in great detail in *The Confidence Plan: How to Build a Stronger You* by one of your authors (Ursiny). In this chapter, we want to present you with a few ideas in each category to help build your self-confidence.

Mental (Thinking Approaches)

Mental (also called cognitive or thinking) strategies are the most common form of confidence-building techniques. These are based on theories of cognitive psychology, which show that what we think has a great impact on our confidence and thus our ability to reach a goal. In fact, some researchers in psychology suggest that the single greatest predictor of your ability to accomplish a task is your belief that you can do it. The psychological term for your belief in your ability to do well in a particular activity is self-efficacy. People with strong self-efficacy have been shown to lead healthier and happier lives. They succeed more often than pessimistic people and achieve their goals more quickly.

To determine your mental confidence, you need look no further than your self-talk. What do you say to yourself each day? When you wake up, do you dread your day, or do you have thoughts about how successful or impactful you are going to be? When you have a challenging sale, do you mentally rehearse all of the things that are going wrong, or do you keep telling yourself to stay tenacious and you will get the sale? While some people can take self-talk too far ("I'm good enough, I'm smart enough, and dog-gone it, people like me"), the science of real-life strategies shows without doubt that our prediction of our own success or failure has a huge impact on what actually happens in the sale and in our lives.

To have confidence as a coach, you must fill your mind with positive and encouraging thoughts. Compare the effectiveness of these two sales professionals attempting to coach a sale.

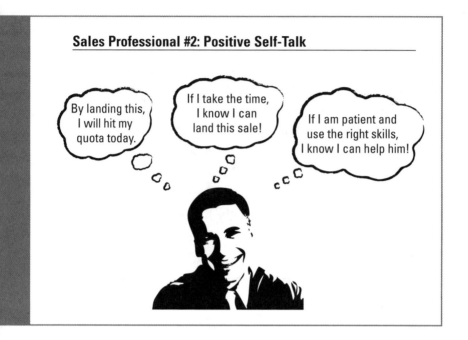

Imagine how differently these two sales professionals would act or coach in that particular sales situation. Who do you believe would be more successful? Is it even a contest? While these examples are a little extreme, they do show what is just plain common sense; what you put in your head will impact what you say, how you say it, and the results that you will get in your approach.

Emotional (Feeling Approaches)

Emotional approaches are different from thinking strategies in that they do not rely on words for their effectiveness. Emotional strategies are those that use nonverbal methods to hit the more primal or subconscious parts of our confidence. These techniques involve the senses of sight, hearing, smell, feeling, and taste. Emotional approaches require more creativity and focus on the right hemisphere of the brain (unlike thinking strategies that are more left-brained in orientation). Sales professionals have known for years the power of tapping into emotional strategies for selling to others. In their book *Storyselling*, authors Scott West and Mitch Anthony show how using stories in sales presentations can trigger both the right and left hemispheres of the prospect and make for a much more persuasive sale. Too many sales professionals ignore emotion for the sake of logic. Human beings act most consistently when logic and emotion both enter the picture in unison.

However, these feeling strategies are also helpful for the sales professional to use on him or herself. Techniques such as hypnosis rely heavily on emotional strategies. Many sales professional are also familiar with NLP or Neuro-Linguistic Programming, which also impacts our emotional confidence at a very deep level. The bottom line is that emotional strategies can require more creativity than thinking strategies, but have the potential to impact confidence and optimism at a very deep and automatic level. Because of biases in western civilization, we can sometimes be more skeptical of emotional approaches as compared to others. Truthfully, the sales professional who does not make use of these powerful techniques will be limited in the level of success that he or she can achieve. For some, they can still be incredibly successful, but they will never realize the potential they could have shown.

So what are some examples of emotion approaches? One of the easier and more accessible techniques is to use music or movies. Take the movie *Top Gun*. Here is a movie that tends to get most people (especially men) pumped up and ready to take on the world. So what makes this movie so powerful? Well it is probably a combination of:

- the script
- the acting
- the scenery
- the sounds of the aircraft, etc.
- the music

You take any of those elements away, and it will be a far less powerful movie. Imagine that movie with less-skilled actors delivering the lines or with a black screen as the only visual or without the music. It just wouldn't do the job! It is the combination of these sights and sounds that have us juiced up and ready to rumble.

Many of us enjoy music and movies, but do we use them strategically to impact our mood and our confidence? One manager for a financial services firm we know instituted movie night in his complex during a particularly difficult time of transition for the firm. This progressive branch office manager would show movies such as *Young Frankenstein, Caddyshack, Mrs. Doubtfire,* and others to financial advisors who wanted to gather after a hard day and just dine and laugh together. As a result of this and other progressive behaviors, he had incredible retention rates with all of his advisors during a time when many were frustrated and disgusted with the firm.

Or take the examples of coaching clients that we have had who used music like "Beethoven's 7th" or "I Will Survive" or "Calling All Angels" to boost their moods after a tough day. Or sales professionals that would feed their minds and hearts with movies that showed people triumphing through challenging times, like *Remember the Titans, The Shawshank Redemption,* or *Defending Your Life.* The right movie or song can hit those parts of us that words simply cannot reach.

Another technique that we have taught in our confidence course is how to use your five senses to build your confidence. In the workshops, we have people imagine what confidence:

- looks like (visualizing it in the moment)
- sounds like (trying to recreate the sound)
- smells like (attempting to fool their olfactory senses to smell it)
- feels like (imagining the texture of confidence)
- tastes like (actually trying to taste success)

An amazing thing happens in our workshops when we do this. People start smiling, then often laughing. They start sitting up in their chairs a little taller. And they are more attentive and engaged for the rest of the workshop. The act of walking through confidence and success using all of their senses actually recharges them and pumps them up. Imagine what this could do if they practiced this on a regular basis or before an important sale. Emotional confidence is crucial in a situation in which you are coaching the sale. Prospects will not tether themselves to anyone who talks a good game but has the "feel" of insecurity.

Behavioral (Action-Oriented Approaches)

What you *do* can have as much impact on your confidence as what you think and how you feel. A sales professional's confidence is highly related to how she confronts feared activities and stretches beyond the comfort zone. The sales professional who avoids uncomfortable activities that will lead to greater success slowly erodes confidence. Avoiding things that we fear actually reinforces the fear. The sales professional who sees on the caller ID that an upset client is calling and fails to pick up the call just became even more fearful of that client. The avoidance basically fed the fear. And when we feed things, they tend to get bigger.

Similarly, most of us have a certain comfort zone. This is the level of behavior and success that feels right to us. If we go below this level of success, then we become uncomfortable and start showing behaviors that will get us back to our previous level. However, did you also know that most of us have a ceiling to this comfort zone? Most of us are uncomfortable if we get too successful. We have a self-limit to our level of accomplishment. In other words, if we get too successful, then we stop doing the behaviors that got us there until we sink back down to our comfortable level of success. This is one reason why many successful sales professionals stop doing the behaviors that made them successful.

We cannot tell you how many times we have run into this. Cold calling was successful, and then they stopped. Holding seminars brought in many new clients, but they don't do it anymore. Certain marketing strategies and approaches were sure winners and they seem to have forgotten their effectiveness. Every time our actions take us back to our comfort zone, we reinforce that zone as the level of success that we will allow ourselves to obtain.

Is comfort your goal? If so, then just do what you are doing. However, if unbelievable success, huge sales, and great impact on others drive you, then you must break out of any fear or comfort habits that you have. You must do the things that frighten you to build your confidence to the next level and most effectively coach the sale. There are two main ways to do this: systematic desensitization and flooding. The chart on the next page describes the difference in these two approaches:

Systematic Desensitization vs. Flooding

	Systematic Desensitization	Flooding
The Approach	Take the thing that you fear and break it down into multiple sequential steps to build yourself up to facing it (often creating five to ten steps). Start with the step you fear least. Once you feel comfortable with achieving that step, then you move on to the next one. Eventually, you will be able to do the thing that makes you fearful or uncomfortable.	Dive in and do the very thing that you fear. Keep doing it long enough until the fear diminishes.
The Theory	By slowly building up to the thing you fear most, you are building your confidence and comfort so that once you confront it, the uncomfortable activity is no longer as big of a fear.	You can only stay fearful or uncomfortable for so much time. If you face something long enough, then eventually your body will quit excreting adrenaline and you will get use to the discomfort.
Benefits	• Is only mildly painful or uncomfortable • Allows a more patient path to progress • Usually involves the additional benefit of learning relaxation techniques	• It is faster • Huge confidence can come from facing your fear quickly
Drawbacks	• It takes time to do • Involves creating multiple steps	• It can be initially very painful

In the end, the method you choose is entirely up to you. Whichever fits with your personality is fine because in the end, both are extremely effective.

Relational (Community Approaches)

Our confidence is not immune to our environment. In fact, the relationships around us can dramatically increase or decrease our level of confidence. If you are surrounded by many negative people or get involved in multiple conflicts, then your confidence will get drained and your ability to effectively coach the sale will be far less effective. This is why your sales manager's (or in financial services, branch office manager's) attitude can be extremely important. It is why the location of your office and who is in the next office should matter to you. It is also why the stability and happiness of your home life can dramatically impact your sales performance.

These two elements of negativity and conflict drain morale, energy, and optimism in a very subversive way. Imagine the sales professional with conflict at home, peers who are always complaining about changes in the home office, and a manager who merely criticizes and demeans rather than supports and challenges. How will he perform compared to the sales professional with a happy home life, peers that are energetic and appropriately competitive, and a manager who sees and calls the person to his highest potential? If the sales professionals are of compatible skill level, then is the comparative performance of these two ever in doubt?

Here are ways you can utilize relational strategies to build your confidence and your coaching.

#1: Surround Yourself with the Right People
Yes, it sounds simple, but it is amazing how many people will continue to hang around with negative people. We have worked with sales professionals to help them eliminate negative friends from their lives. Now, we are not talking about friends who are going through a tough time and need your support, but rather those individuals who are chronically negative and tend to bring you and others down. You can identify them easily because usually you are trying to help them *more* than they are trying to help themselves. In addition, we have helped companies develop a "zero tolerance for negativity." We have helped them utilize this principle in their interviewing process and create performance reviews that are heavily weighted on attitude. Again, negativity is not to be confused with venting or problem-solving. People who vent are "negative with a purpose." The purpose is to let go of the bad feelings and move on. Negative people are just negative to be negative. Also, people who identify challenges and help solve them are invaluable to a sales organization. However, the big difference is that negative people come to you complaining about problems; those who problem solve bring you both challenges and potential solutions. While it is difficult to completely avoid negative people, you have many choices including confronting, ignoring, and walking away from them. You do not need to be a victim of their negative energy.

#2: Learn to Face and Deal with Conflict
The fact that most people tend to either avoid conflict or deal with it poorly led one of your authors (Ursiny) to write the book *The Coward's Guide to Conflict*. The book explores

why people avoid conflict, what causes conflict, and tactics for creating positive and impactful communication. Many sales professionals avoid conflict at all costs. This can create problem situations such as:

✓ over-promising to a demanding client
✓ failure to deal with people in the home office who drain you
✓ hanging around others with whom you do not want to be friends
✓ withdrawal from a relationship with a significant other
✓ difficulty saying "no"
✓ trying to please a demanding manager
✓ fear of rejection (so failing to close the sale)
✓ physical symptoms such as heartburn, ulcers, headaches, etc.
✓ failure to institute change in your life

One of the biggest reasons that people avoid conflict is because of anticipatory anxiety. This anxiety is the nervousness you feel as you anticipate doing something. Most individuals feel anticipatory anxiety before a conflict because they imagine all of the ways that the conflict might go poorly before they meet with the person. Not only does this drain them, but it also creates an atmosphere of tension in the interaction that may actually contribute to the confrontation going poorly. Those who walk into a conflict imagining a positive outcome and a variety of win-win solutions have a much better chance at creating a good outcome from the meeting.

Other sales professionals have the opposite problem. Instead of avoiding conflict, they have a proactive hand in creating it. Because the sales profession draws many driven people, it also is full of those that have not learned how to separate drive from aggression. While we are huge proponents of creating healthy competition in sales, we have also seen the devastation that can come from arrogant and narcissistic sales professionals who care about nothing but the sale. Many of these individuals can get pretty far in their success just because of the amount of time, tenacity, and force they are putting behind it. But again, they will never realize their full potential until they learn how to create winning situations for all involved and form more lasting relationships.

The role of relationships in sales continues to grow in importance. Sales professionals with similar products are often competing for the same sale. In that situation, the confident sales professional who creates an aura of safety for the prospect is sure to win over the arrogant sales professional who is forceful in approach. Learning to deal with objections, challenges, and hesitancies in the sale is an important part of the coaching process. Often, this takes adapting our natural style to the behavioral style of the prospect.

#3: Develop a Positive Relationship with Your Manager

We realize that some of our readers will be entrepreneurs with no real manager. You can just read into this section the importance of a good relationship with yourself! However, readers with a difficult sales manager realize how difficult the wrong relationship can be in your career. Conflict skills are crucial for dealing with your manager. At times, you will have competing goals and this will create conflict. By dealing with the conflict successfully, you can build a strong advocate in your manager. If you fail to deal well with the conflict, then you are just causing more pain and trouble for yourself down the road. Always keep in mind ways to create a "win-win" relationship with your manager.

In financial services, the most successful advisors routinely look at their client list and divide them into certain categories of clients. A certain percentage of their clients are often referred to a new beginning advisor or to a clearinghouse part of the firm. These clients are often assessed on their financial impact on the advisor's bottom line. However, most top-performing advisors also take into account the relationship with the client.

In other words, a client may have a significant amount of money invested with the advisor, but if the client is negative, high maintenance, and draining, then the client is often referred to someone else. Why would a top performer let go of this income stream? Well, very simply, he knows that there is a price tag on the amount of energy the client is allowed to drain from the advisor. A high maintenance, negative client is often not worth the price she is pulling from the advisor.

Less confident advisors have difficulty letting go of profitable clients. The smartest advisors who believe in abundance are able to take the temporary loss of money in order to recapture the time and energy pulled from them by the client. They are optimistic about their ability to use that energy to generate additional revenue from a client with whom they enjoy working. So you just need to ask yourself a simple question, "Do I believe in abundance or will I hold on to clients who slap me around every chance they get?"

#5: Give Back to Others

Some interesting studies in the area of life happiness and satisfaction suggest that altruistic acts (unselfish acts of giving to others) have an incredibly powerful impact on our confidence. The best coaches do what they do not just for the money (although that tends to come) but for the joy of positively impacting others. They realize that significance is more important than success, and ironically, success often comes when you focus more on significance. Sure, coaching the sale is about making the sale, but at the core it is about impacting others' lives in a positive and meaningful way. You really care if the sale is the most beneficial for them. You are willing to let go of profit if it is the right thing for the client. Your integrity is more important than the dollar bill. Insecure people believe that they need to make the sale happen in order to be successful. Confident and optimistic sales professionals know that there are plenty of people to sell to and that the cost of a bad sale is not worth the toll on your integrity. People who live with integrity live with energy. People who will do anything to get by are on the temporary fuel that comes with momentary success.

We recently had the privilege of interviewing the fifty top salespeople for the Midwest region of a Fortune 500 firm. Part of the interview process was to determine strategies for helping the sales professionals deal with the recent transition that was occurring from a merger. An additional goal was to gather best practices. What made these top sales professionals so good? Why were they the top fifty in a firm of thousands? As we explored all of the different factors that made them successful, the most common element concerned their treatment of their clients. Common responses were:

- I will always do what is best for my client
- I truly care about my clients
- I will sacrifice momentary gain for my client's sake
- I love my clients
- I will bend over backwards to take care of my clients

To be the best sales coach you can be, you must focus on giving back to others. You must believe in aiding others over making a profit. And you must know that there is not a dollar price on your integrity.

Spiritual (Life Purpose and Mission Approaches)

Many have experienced the fragility of confidence. Our thoughts, feelings, behaviors, and relationships can be fleeting and vulnerable. However, there is one factor at the core of confidence that no one can impact unless *you* let them. Obviously, this is spiritual confidence. We are using spiritual in the broadest sense of the word to refer to living your life mission and purpose. When you are fully connected to the reason why you exist on this planet and what you are to accomplish, then nothing can shake your confidence. Self-betrayal is a form of harm that no one else can do to you. You can only do it to yourself. When you are connected to your mission, then no one can steal your optimism. For example, you can always lose a sale, but as long as you are living with the purpose of impacting other lives for the positive, then a lost sale is only a momentary glitch in your day. If your mission is to honor God in your everyday life, then a lost sale has no impact on how you feel for the day. If your purpose is to love your family with all of your heart, then a challenging sales day is only a distraction to your mission.

Only you can determine your purpose and mission. And only you can steal your confidence away by failing to follow what you were called to do.

The book *The Confidence Plan: How to Build a Stronger You* is full of exercises for each of the five areas of building confidence. For the purpose of this book, we offer a few easier methods below.

EXERCISE: Mental Exercise

Fill your mind with thoughts and memories that will motivate you on challenging days. For example, if you know that you are about to face a challenging day, there are many very effective mental strategies for preparing yourself. A few examples are:

- Run a mental replay of your top previous sale, analyzing and reinforcing in your mind all of the things you did right and allowing yourself to relive the success (another way to do this is to keep a success file of times when things go well, you get recognition, promotions, career milestones, etc., that you can physically open when you need a boost).

- Remind yourself of your true beliefs such as, "I love challenges and will confidently face anything that crosses my path today," instead of allowing the challenge to distract you from what you believe about your identity.

- Mentally reframe the challenge into a game or a competition that gets your pulse beating with excitement rather than fear.

- Focus on all of the things in your life for which you are grateful, those things that will be unaffected by the outcome of the challenge and thus give you a "safety net."

Put your strategy here:

_____

_____

_____

_____

Try to have this thought first thing in the morning when you wake up.

_____

_____

_____

_____

EXERCISE: Emotional Exercise

Use your five senses to describe what confidence is for you. Write your responses in the blanks below:

Confidence looks like (describe something visually):

_____

_____

Confidence sounds like (describe something you can hear):

_____

_____

Confidence smells like (describe something using your olfactory senses):

_____

_____

Confidence feels like (describe something by its texture):

_____

_____

Confidence tastes like (describe something using your sense of taste):

_____

_____

Now practice these senses when you are facing a sales situation in which you want to have great confidence and be successful.

EXERCISE: Behavioral Exercise

Pick a behavior, action, or situation that you have been avoiding. What big/uncomfortable (but safe) step do you need to take to go to your next level of success? Write your answer here:

_____

_____

_____

_____

Now pick either a systematic desensitization or flooding approach to it. If you choose flooding, then just do it, and stay in the situation until it is no longer uncomfortable for you. If you choose systematic desensitization, then write five steps below that will slowly build you up to the behavior. For example, if the behavior is approaching a high net worth prospect who intimidates you with a new financial planning tool, then you might do the following steps:

Step #1: Practice the tool on yourself

Step #2: Practice the tool with a friend or colleague

Step #3: Practice the tool with a client with whom you feel extremely comfortable

Step #4: Practice the tool with a lower net worth client with whom you have some discomfort

Step #5: Set up the appointment with the high net worth client

Write your steps below:

Step #1:

_____

_____

_____

_____

Step #2:

_____

_____

_____

_____

Step #3:

_____

_____

_____

_____

Step #4:

_____

_____

_____

_____

Step #5:

_____

_____

_____

_____

Go ahead and start with step one and build your confidence to move to step five and beyond.

EXERCISE: Relational Exercise

What is a conflict or conversation that you have been avoiding with your manager, a peer, a friend, or a significant other? Do a plus and minus analysis of avoiding the behavior and make a decision whether your avoidance is draining your energy.

The conversation:

_____

_____

_____

_____

	Positives	Negatives
Facing the conversation		
Avoiding the conversation		

What will you do about this conversation?

_____

_____

_____

_____

EXERCISE: Spiritual Exercise

This is a shorter version of an exercise that can be found in *The Confidence Plan: How to Build a Stronger You*. Use this format to gain insight into your purpose and mission:

The purpose of my life and work is to (list the objectives; what you want to accomplish):

_____

_____

_____

_____

I will do this for (list who will be the recipients of your life purpose):

_____

_____

_____

_____

I will accomplish this by (list the behaviors or activities that you will do to live out your purpose):

_____

_____

_____

_____

Chapter 7

Next Steps:

Becoming a Coach

"A great deal of talent is lost to the world for want of a little courage. Every day sends to their graves obscure men whose timidity prevented them from making a first effort. "

—Sydney Smith

Overview

So are you ready to unite consultative selling and coaching to cross that critical yard? We realize that for some of you, this evolution may be a minor one in which you are only changing a small percentage of what you are already doing. In addition, you might be gathering and using a few additional tips that you found in this book. For others, we realize that the shift is a dramatic one for which you may have some hesitations. What is wonderful is that steps to transform are similar to the steps you take the prospect through for a buying decision. You need to:

- discover your goals as a sales professional
- discuss or explore your options (either in your head or with someone else)
- decide which approach is best for you

Tales from the Playing Field

I was recently working with one of my company's wholesalers. We were in the parking lot preparing for a sales call with an extremely successful financial advisor who we will call Frank. The wholesaler was on a mission to sell Frank on our new variable annuity product. We went up to Frank's office and my wholesaler friend opened the conversation with all of the merits of our product and why Frank should start recommending this product to his clients. After ten minutes, the wholesaler stopped and asked Frank what he thought about the product. Frank just stared at each of us for a few seconds and then said, "I have *never* in my thirteen years as an advisor bought a variable annuity. I don't believe in them and I will never buy one."

This was, of course, a complete disaster. I quickly jumped into the conversation and asked, "So tell me Frank, what are you working on right now?" He responded by talking about the fact that he had just completed an analysis on his clients' portfolios and that he saw that there was a hole for his clients in small-cap values. Therefore, we immediately shifted our discussion to our small cap values product. The interaction became a true discussion at that point and went from the feeling of tension to one of collaboration. At the end of the conversation, we asked Frank for a decision. He saw the benefits of our product and was confident that it would serve his clients well.

Thankfully, we had a previous long-term relationship with Frank. That is the *only* reason that we got the chance to switch to a topic he cared about and a product that he would buy. Had we started the conversation with something like "I'm prepared to talk with you today about one of our products, but I wanted to find out first what you are working on these days," then the conversation would have gotten to the right topic immediately rather than wasting time and almost destroying a sale. We almost destroyed the sale from the very beginning. We could have also sabotaged our success by not moving to a positive feeling of discussion or by failing to ask Frank for a decision. The sales process can blow up in your face if you do it incorrectly. By quickly switching to our 3D model, we were able to turn this near disaster into a profitable success.

Principles

As we asked you in the overview, are you ready to unite consultative selling and coaching? Whether the transformation is minor or major, do you want to turn your studying of this book into critical yard action? If you have any hesitation, then you simply need to walk yourself through similar steps that you take the prospect through for a buying decision. To transform, you need to adapt the 3D coaching model to:
  • discover your goals as a sales professional
  • discuss or explore your options (either in your head or with someone else)
  • decide which approach is best for you

Discover Your Goals as a Sales Professional

What drives you? What motivates you to wake up each morning and take on the day? Your drives and motivators are crucial to understand in order to aid your transformation (whether it be small or large). Face it, we are bombarded every day with information of what we "should" and "should not" be doing. We should lose weight, we shouldn't open computer attachments from people we don't know, we should exercise, we shouldn't drink coffee, we should spend more time with our families, we shouldn't work so hard, we should perform better. The list never stops.

In a life full of information, strategies like the ones presented in this book can get lost in the shuffle. One way to ensure that you keep with the program is to consciously tie in the principles from this book that resonated with you with your goals and motivations. For example, if your main goal of living on this planet is to improve the lives of those who come in contact with you, how does this coaching style fit with that mission? The more you connect the information with your emotions and desires, the more you will practice.

Discuss or Explore Your Options (Either in Your Head or with Someone Else)

As coaches, we do not expect you to follow our model perfectly. In fact, it may be even better for you if you tweak the model more to fit your personality and goals. Have a discussion with yourself about your likes and dislikes of this model. What fits for you and what would fit even better? Write out some of your thoughts so that you can look them over and really explore the path that will be best for you. You might even build a plus and minus list of what really stood out to you. Even better than trying to do all of this in your head is talking with someone else about it. Hire a coach or grab a friend to walk through the book with you.

Work together to wrap your hands around the model and really think it through. Either way, make sure you discuss these principles and strategies so that they become your own or you build something even better for yourself than what we had to offer.

Decide Which Approach Is Best for You

As coaches, we trust that you are a capable and talented human being who is an expert in your own life. We know that you can make the right decision about this process given all of your other characteristics, habits, and skills. We just want to make sure that you *make a decision*! Don't let this just be another nice read that goes on your bookshelf with the promise to yourself that someday you will get back to it. Decide now to:

- dump it (not use the coaching the sale model)
- adapt it (pull a few strategies and principles to add to your current approach)
- do it (fully engage in the coaching the sale model)

Make this decision conscious and make it now.

Your Next Thirty Days

For any change in habit, it is crucial to start fast, start hard, and stay consistent. The exercises that follow at the end of this chapter are there to help you build an action plan to move your "skill shifts" forward. We strongly encourage you to do the following to maximize your chances of making the return on investment with this book reach incredible heights:

Start practicing today. Do not wait for next week; do not put the book aside and say you will come back to it. Do it now.

If you did not do all of the exercises, then go back and do them. We know how you feel—we often don't like to do them either, but this is how you will get the most out of this product.

Get an accountability partner—find another sales professional who might benefit from these principles and discuss the book together. Meet on a weekly basis for the first month to discuss how you utilized the techniques in this book and form new actions for the next week. This will help you be accountable to fully put the strategies into practice.

Set a daily reminder system to keep your focus on this process. Do this by putting a note up on your computer, building a cheat sheet for techniques, putting a note on your mirror at home, having a loved one ask you how the coaching process is going, etc.

Review the Appendix in this book that summarizes the entire 3D model.

Reread this book.

EXERCISE: Building an Initial Action Plan (Shorter Version)

Answer the following questions to start the process of transforming to the 3D coaching model:

What is the most important principle, technique, or strategy that stood out to you from this book?

_____

_____

_____

_____

How will you put this principle into action?

_____

_____

_____

_____

How will you stay accountable to this?

_____

_____

_____

_____

By when will you check back in with yourself to see if you have made progress?

_____

_____

_____

_____

| EXERCISE: | Building a More Extensive Action Plan (Full Version) |

For those high achievers, go chapter by chapter, review this book, and answer the following questions to fully commit to transforming into a coach in your sales process:

Chapter 1

Review the assessment that you did at the end of chapter 1. Now that you have completed the book, what areas do you need to continue to focus on to transform your style to a coaching the sale style?

_____

_____

_____

_____

_____

How would you like people to describe you after you have coached the sale with them?

_____

_____

_____

_____

_____

What is a measurable action step to make this happen, and by when will you do it?

_____

_____

_____

_____

_____

Chapter 2

Looking over the skill sets of an effective coach, in what skills would you like to grow?

_____

_____

_____

_____

_____

_____

How will you go about improving these skills (reading books, going to training, hiring a coach, etc.)?

_____

_____

_____

_____

_____

_____

By when will you do it?

_____

_____

_____

_____

_____

_____

_____

Chapter 3

Review the TBOP process, along with the reflective review. How and when will you put this process into practice?

_____

_____

_____

_____

_____

_____

To whom will you be accountable?

_____

_____

_____

_____

_____

How will you celebrate your success when the process works?

_____

_____

_____

_____

_____

_____

Chapter 4

Review the Discuss phase. How else could you use storyboarding to improve your sales performance and process?

_____

_____

_____

_____

_____

_____

How often might you revisit your three-point play to ensure that you are up to date and using the most effective solutions possible?

_____

_____

_____

_____

_____

_____

How will you remind yourself of this on a regular basis?

_____

_____

_____

_____

_____

_____

Chapter 5

Review the Decide phase. What are some actions you could put in place to help improve your ability to coach prospects to a decision?

_____

_____

_____

_____

_____

_____

How will you practice these?

_____

_____

_____

_____

_____

When will you start?

_____

_____

_____

_____

_____

Chapter 6

Which of the paths to confidence would you like to work on the most (mental, emotional, behavioral, relational, or spiritual)?

_____

_____

_____

_____

_____

_____

How will you go about doing this?

_____

_____

_____

_____

_____

By when will you do this and how will you know that you have succeeded?

_____

_____

_____

_____

_____

_____

EXERCISE: Do It!

The time for writing is done. Go do it! Good luck as you continue to grow in your effectiveness and impact as a sales professional and as a coach!

Summary Outline of the 3D Coaching Conversation

Taking you through the 3D model across three different chapters can be a little intimidating. Therefore, let's review in summary form the three parts of the process.

Discover Phase—Reflect and Reveal
Make small talk to build an emotional connection and increase collaboration with your prospect

Use the TBOP formula to fully understand your prospect's needs, following a process of revealing his or her perspectives and reflecting these perspectives back

Transitional Opener—Move the conversation to the goal at hand
✓ Start with a statement of confidence, willingness, and preparedness
✓ State the benefit to the client of using a coaching approach
✓ Discover priorities and end with verbalized agreement of goals

Benefits—Help your prospect paint a picture of the benefits of reaching his or her goals to increase the motivation to make a decision about the purchase

Obstacles—Reveal and reflect what has stopped your prospects from reaching their stated goals (and making a purchase) in the past

Plans—Reflect and reveal previous and current plans for purchasing
✓ Use the coaching tool of TEAM to adapt to the prospect's style to increase the feelings of comfort and trust
✓ Segue to the Discuss phase using the reflective review to smoothly check and demonstrate your full understanding of the client's perspectives and motives

If I understand you correctly, you are saying that you want _____ (name goal) because it will give you _____ (name benefits) and that you have been stopped in the past because _____ (name obstacles) when you have done _____ (name plans). Is that right (get agreement)? Okay, well what I would like to do then is for us to take your thoughts and some of my ideas and see if we can collaborate on a good solution for you. How open do you feel to looking at that right now?

Once you get agreement, you move to the Discuss phase. If you get resistance, then you need to backtrack in the model to see what you missed or make the decision that the prospect is not ready to buy.

Discuss Phase—Share/Pause/Agree
✓ Use the coaching tool of storyboarding to prepare categories for the solutions that your product provides

✓ Use the three-point play to connect solutions to goals using "oil" or smooth questions

Share point #1
  ✓ Connect it back to the initial goals
  ✓ Check in with question

Share point #2
  ✓ Connect it back to the initial goals
  ✓ Check in with question

Share point #3
  ✓ Connect it back to the initial goals
  ✓ Check in with a question
  ✓ Segue to the Decide phase using the reflective review

It sounds like we are in agreement on (Point #1, Point #2, Point #3) matching up well with (client's goal or goals). Is that correct?

Decide Phase—Form Collaboration and Accountability
  ✓ Use the CAT model for deciding

Collaborative Close—Determine if a decision has been made using an open ended question

Action Steps—Work with the client to form the next steps in the process

Timing and Follow Up—Determine an accountability plan to measure progress

Use the coaching tool APPA (Acknowledge, Pursue, Provide, Acceptance) to graciously deal with client objections or hesitations.

Again, it may seem like a lot at one sitting, but take your time to really walk through each step. The payoff will be worth it.

Index

About the Authors

Your authors want you to be successful at uniting consultative selling and coaching skills. Please let us know your success stories or request additional tools, workshops, or individualized coaching help for yourself or your team by contacting us.

Tim Ursiny

Tim Ursiny, PhD, CBC, RCC is the CEO of Advantage Coaching & Training (www.advantagecoaching.com). He is a coach/trainer specializing in helping people reach peak performance, great relationships, and personal happiness.

Dr. Tim regularly speaks for Fortune 500 companies who want workshops that are practical yet entertaining. He also coaches CEOs, executives, sales professionals, and others on a variety of subjects related to performance and life satisfaction. Dr. Tim's previous books include *The Confidence Plan: How to Build a Stronger You, The Coach's Handbook,* and *The Coward's Guide to Conflict,* which is currently in its third printing and has been translated into several foreign languages. He is currently writing a series of books called *What Top Performers Know about...* around such topics as change, conflict, networking, attitude, and public speaking.

He lives Wheaton, Illinois, with his wife, Marla, and his three sons, Zach, Colton, and Vance. Dr. Tim can be reached at Drtim@advantagecoaching.com.

Gary DeMoss

Gary DeMoss is the director of Van Kampen Consulting, which provides communication and relationship-skills training to financial advisors. Gary has been with Van Kampen for twenty-four years. He began his career with the company by starting and directing their national sales. He was later named director of marketing and in 1998 started Van Kampen Consulting. Gary is a keynote speaker, seminar leader, and consultant to advisors who want to build their affluent client base, and he was recently selected as a platform speaker at the 2003 Million Dollar Round Table conference.

He is the coauthor of the book *The Financial Professional's Guide to Persuading 1 or 1,000*, which helps advisors learn the science and art of delivering more powerful client presentations both one-on-one and in group settings.

Prior to joining Van Kampen, Gary was with Procter & Gamble in sales management. He has a BS in business from Miami University in Oxford, Ohio.

You can reach Gary at demossg@vankampen.com.

Jim Morel

Jim Morel is the founder/chairman and CEO of Jam Consulting Group, Inc., a sales and management consulting firm. In addition to his work as an executive sales coach and consultant, Jim is a sought-after keynote speaker. Prior to founding JAM Consulting Group, Inc., he worked for thirty years in financial services in several areas, including senior management as president of a broker dealer company, commissioned sales, and international and national sales management. Over the years, Jim has successfully rebuilt and re-energized hundreds of sales teams struggling at one time or another.

Jim holds undergraduate and graduate degrees in education, psychology, and science from Purdue University in Lafayette, Indiana. He is on numerous advisory boards and involved with many nonprofit organizations. Jim lives in St. Charles, Illinois, with his wife, Sherry. He has three children, Tom, Kaleen, and Marques, along with six grandchildren.

You can reach Jim at moreljam@aol.com.